TEN CHURCH GROWTH PRINCIPLES

"Empowering Your Church To Grow"

Rev. Chester B. Tollette

Copyright © 2011 by Chester B. Tollette
Los Angeles, California
All rights reserved
Printed and Bound in the United States of America

Published and Distributed by:
Professional Publishing House
1425 W. Manchester Ave., Suite B
Los Angeles, California 90047
(323) 750-3592
Drrosie@aol.com

Cover design: Kevin Allen
First printing Sept. 2011
978-0-9834444-7-3
10987654321

No part of this book may be reproduced, stored in a retrieval system or transmitted in any form or by any means without the prior written permission of the publisher—except by a reviewer who may quote brief passages in a review to be printed in a newspaper, magazine, or journal.

Direct inquiries to Rev. Tollette at tollette@aol.com.

What People Are Saying About Rev. Chester B. Tollette

"I've found Century Church Growth Center to be unlimited on its resourcefulness. Our congregation has experienced exceptional growth through the use of materials, strategies, and the development of cell groups."

Rev. James Markham, Pastor
Emmanuel Temple Church, Victorville, CA

"Pastor Tollette has developed effective strategies in helping churches to maximize their God-ordained potential establishing churches on the authority of God's Word. Our application of soul winning, cell groups, and staff development has made a warm and thriving church body."

Bishop George McKinney
Stephens Church of God in Christ, San Diego, CA

"Through Rev. Tollette's teachings on sound biblical methods of church growth and the sharing of methods and materials, he has aided Carter Temple in reaching many more souls for Christ."

Bishop Henry Williamson
7th Episcopal District, CME Church

"Pastor and laypersons were greatly pleased with the presentation by Rev. Tollette. The use of graphs and statistics gave meaning and substance in presenting basic information useful for growth and development of churches. The information was presented in such a way that any church would benefit and experience growth. We highly recommend Rev. Tollette as a resource and consultant in evangelism."

Rev. Otis Gordon
Episcopal Director of Christian Education
3rd Episcopal District AME Church

Contents

Acknowledgments 5
About the Author 7
Preface 9
Introduction 15
Chapter 1: Conditions for Church Growth 27
Chapter 2: Evangelism 44
Chapter 3: The Call to Preach 61
Chapter 4: Entering the Itinerate Ministry 69
Chapter 5: Ministry at Riverside 88
Chapter 6: Social Ministries in Action 104
Chapter 7: Developing Vision 145
Chapter 8: Leadership—Making It Happen 162
Chapter 9: Worship 180
Chapter 10: Church Administration for Today 190
Chapter 11: Prayer 207
Chapter 12: Assimilating New Members 217
Conclusion 225
Bibliography 229

Acknowledgments

This book is somewhat like a story which takes place in a number of locations where I have learned about "growing" churches. Many people have assisted me in writing this book, and some were not even aware that they were playing a role in doing so. A large number of people, too numerous to mention, have played a significant part in the experiences of my pastorate in consultations in many churches.

First, I must thank my wife, Shirley, for her support, patience, and sharing some of my enthusiasm as I read and reread this document. Her suggestions were extremely valuable throughout this endeavor. I am indebted to my brother, Rev. Sanford Tollette, who has been a mentor to me throughout my ministry.

It was the late Bishop Nathaniel Lindsey who brought about a fundamental change in my ministry. Bishop Lindsey introduced me to professors of church growth at Fuller Seminary, and I subsequently pursued a curriculum in church growth and consultation. Bishop Lindsey appointed me Episcopal Director of Evangelism, which afforded me the opportunity to gain experience working with churches in a broader area.

Dr. Karen Salibak, a new acquaintance, became interested soon after learning that I was writing a book. Karen displayed an unusual fascination regarding this undertaking. Weekly meetings were scheduled which focused on time management to assure certain chapters or sections were completed as planned. The meetings proved to be most helpful as this was an area where there was a personal need.

A very special thanks to Pastor James Markham who succeeded me at my first pastoral appointment. We have maintained a strong bond. Pastor Markham has had a strong prayer life, and he brought to this production a powerful emphasis on prayer. As a result of this relationship, my personal prayer life became much stronger, and I attribute this to the model that Rev. Markham practiced. We spent many evenings in prayer and discussing how to organize the ideas to be included in the book.

My cousin Don Oliver and I walked each morning. Don shared many practical ideas about writing, and many of these ideas were incorporated in this book. I must thank him for his insights and suggestions.

Finally, I want to give a very special thanks to my publisher, Dr. Rosie Milligan, who has gone far beyond expectations in the process of publishing this book.

About the Author

Rev. Chester B. Tollette is a certified church growth consultant (church development) by the Fuller Institute of Evangelism (only two Blacks have this certification) of Pasadena, California. He has served as senior pastor, youth pastor, Episcopal Director of Evangelism and church development. He has also served as prison chaplain for the State of California for a period of seven years. He was appointed as a special recruiting officer for the United States Naval Academy, Annapolis, Maryland.

Among his many accomplishments, Rev. Tollette has served the Los Angeles City School District as a classroom teacher, a master training teacher for the University of Southern California, a mental health counselor, and math coordinator. He retired early to devote full time to ministry. He has also been appointed drug commissioner for the city of Richmond, California. Rev. Tollette was also appointed commissioner representing Contra Costa County in developing a six-county regional government. He has received leadership training and community organizing principles by the Industrial Areas Foundation. (President Obama was trained in community organizing by this organization.)

Rev. Tollette has often been the keynote speaker at church growth conferences and has taught in several convocations. He has conducted workshops and seminars for churches of various denominations across the United States, including Alaska. His expertise in church development has benefited pastors and denominational leaders immensely.

Education & Professional Preparation

- University of Arkansas, Pine Bluff, AR

- California State University, Los Angeles, BA, Education

- Loyola University NDA One-year Grant Mexican History and Culture

- California State University LA, MA, Counseling

- Fuller Seminary, Pasadena CA, Fuller Evangelism Association, certified as a church consultant

Preface

As you look at the title of this book, *Ten Church Growth Principles*, you may be wondering why another church growth book is on the market since there have been hundreds of books written on this subject for the past 40 years. That's a legitimate question. Most of the books available on this subject today are written on the basis of theory.

According to recent statistics, 70 percent of our communities are made up of people who are unchurched. These numbers are alarming. When we encourage and entice people to become disciples of Jesus Christ, it serves us all well. Our communities would be safer if more people were disciples. It is my belief that by growing our churches' membership, a paradigm shift for the better would take place in our communities and in the world.

Children learn principles in church school that linger with them forever, thusly causing them to be better citizens. Think about the lessons learned that have helped shape your life in a productive and positive manner. Lessons such as: Do unto others as you would have them do unto you, honor your mother and father so that it will be well with you and your days may be long, learn to pray, and bless your food before eating (thereby creating a grateful heart). Social skills are learned in Sunday School, youth Bible Study, and vacation Bible school.

Many great orators and singers have come out of the church, where their gifts were encouraged and nurtured. Remember in the old days when we were children, even when we messed up when reciting our little speech or singing our song, or when we forgot our part in a play, you would hear one of the mothers say, "That's all right, baby, you did good," and everybody would give you a big hand clap, even when you never got a word out of your mouth, even when you got up and started crying and never said a word? They still clapped for you.

When I reflect on my growing up in the church, I know without a doubt that a healthy church serves us well. I often hear people make statements such as: "Their parents ought to teach them better," "Where are their parents?" etc. There is an assumption that every child came from a home where there were a mother and a father present, and unfortunately, this is far from the truth these days. The church is the first extension of a family and socialization for a child. He/she attends church before attending preschool, Head Start school, etc. If we can grow our church both in numbers and spirituality via making disciples out of the adults, the children will be included in the church number growth and we would have better students in the classrooms, at the parks, and in the community as a whole.

Our community will not get better until we increase its members' spiritual outlook. I contend that growing a healthy church is the solution to many of our problems and challenges that we face today. We must make growing the church a priority. Church growth will benefit us all. This book, *Ten Church Growth Principles: Empowering Your Church To Grow*, is written to encourage and empower the church to seek growth.

Let's take a look at the historical perspective of church growth.

Historical Perspective

Surprisingly, the church growth movement did not start in America. This idea was brought to the United States by Donald McGavran approximately 65 years ago. During his 60 years of service as a missionary in India, he formulated principles of church growth and applied them in his missionary work in that country. He initially attempted to articulate the insights in traditional language such as "missions" and "evangelism." However, he became aware that these terms weren't working very well because they had lost the original impact because they were used indiscriminately.

In order to define a more useful way of what he was saying, he took two common words, "church" and "growth," and put them together. Church growth is a technical phrase meaning more than "church" and more than "growth." Church growth simply means all that is involved in bringing men and women into fellowship with Jesus Christ and into responsible church membership.

Many people have taken the attitude that church growth is just a numbers game. I will state emphatically that this is not true, certainly not in the context how it is commonly understood. We must understand that numbers actually represent people. We count the number of people in attendance each Sunday, we count how many people are on the church roll, and sometimes we even count how many members are tithing. Perhaps we should also count how many members are leaving our churches.

Some of our leaders have even made public statements such as, "If they aren't satisfied with the way we do things, there is a church down the street that may satisfy them." Statements of this type would seem to be an invitation for people to leave. In fact, many people are taking notice of this advice and are actually "going down the street."

God must be interested in numbers because He named a book in the Old Testament "Numbers." It is ironic that we seldom hear pastors with large numbers in their congregations complain about having too many members. It seems that the complaints against church growth come from those who do not have very many members.

One of the most significant contributions of the church growth movement is the emphasis on making disciples. The goal of church growth is not just for people to make decisions and become good church members. The ultimate purpose of the church is to make disciples, and one of the by-products of this process is growth. Making disciples does require a considerable amount of one's time for training.

Society is not static; it is always in a state of constant change. Changes are taking place all around us, but we as the church are not able to perceive them. These changes have made a great impact on our basic institutions such as the church, school, and family.

Usually our first instinct is to resist the very changes which may make the church more effective in reaching the lost. So often the church is the last institution to make the changes which are necessary to meet the needs inherent in our society today. Let us be reminded that someone once said that the sands of time are strewn with the bones of institutions that *refused to change.*

Introduction

As you have decided to read this book, you will understand the focal point of the information is primarily for churches with memberships less than 250 members. A secondary focus of this book is on black denominations and independent churches. As a certified church consultant, I will introduce and utilize ten church growth principles and methods in solving problems which affect the health of a church. My involvement does not have any bearing upon the theology, polity, or core values of churches or denominations.

During my many years of consulting, I have observed that many of our churches are effective in worship, but are usually lacking in making disciples. Pastors and members must be innovative and creative in attracting members to the church in this postmodern society.

Research shows that the average worship attendance in American churches is approximately 50 persons in the 11:00 A.M. service on Sundays. I believe that every church should reach its potential in carrying out the mandate of making disciples of the unsaved or unchurched persons in the community it serves, regardless of its size. There are always needs in our communities which are not being met. Obviously, it is a great challenge for a small congregation to make a significant impact on community needs. Small congregations are limited in human and financial resources to organize and maintain ministries which meet the growing needs in their community.

Even with limitations of resources, congregations must remain faithful in following the mandates of Christ. Whereas church growth principles apply to all churches, my objective is to reach churches, whether they have an Episcopal or Congregational form of government such as Methodist, Baptist, Church of God in Christ, or independent.

Most of our churches do an outstanding job in offering dynamic worship services, but I have observed that there is a serious lack in teaching discipleship. We must remember that Jesus said in the 28th chapter of the Gospel of Matthew, "Go ye therefore, and make **disciples** of all nations…"

The million-dollar question is why are we not as effective as we should be in making disciples?

Principle #1: Churches grow when there is a strong commitment to discipleship

At the age of 35, I started my own business of manufacturing boats. For 14 years, I operated this business in Pasadena, California. These were some of my most adventurous times. Tragedy ended this endeavor abruptly, but God often uses tragedies for the good. This was a very valuable experience as I learned much about management, and business relationships, and supervision of workers. I also learned to be creative and innovative in solving business problems. All of these skills have been useful in my career of teaching, management, and consultation.

During this period, Bishop Nathaniel L. Linsey was assigned as the presiding bishop of the Ninth Episcopal District of the Christian Methodist Episcopal Church. Before being elected bishop, he held the position of General Secretary of Evangelism. Bishop Linsey immediately appointed me to the position of Episcopal Director of Evangelism of the Ninth Episcopal District. It was a full-time position housed in the Episcopal headquarters. This was the first time this position was filled as a full-time paid position in this denomination.

One morning when arriving at my office, the bishop informed me that we had an appointment in Pasadena, California, with some individuals who were involved in evangelism and church growth. When we arrived at Fuller Seminary, we were hosted by a professor of church growth and two other officials of the Fuller Evangelical Association. As a result of this visit, I eventually enrolled in Fuller Seminary and was certified as a church growth consultant by the Fuller Evangelical Association. All of the life skills that I had learned previously were adaptable to my work as a pastor and consultant.

I accepted the call to ministry late in life at the age of 42 years old. Though I was older than most, I had a distinct advantage because of my life experiences which were real assets.

After years as a successful pastor and serving as a church consultant, many people suggested that I write a book which would be helpful to pastors and laypersons who would like to see their churches grow. I never took their suggestions seriously because I never thought of myself as a writer.

First, I must confess that I have a bias concerning church growth. My position is validated by the knowledge learned in seminars, conferences, and years of experience consulting with churches utilizing principles of church growth. The principles learned in this curriculum are the basis of effectiveness in pastoral ministry. Church growth principles do not in any way change, or alter, the polity or doctrine of churches or denominations. Therefore, these principles and methods are universal and may be applied to any Christian tradition.

As you look at the title *Ten Church Growth Principles: Empowering Your Church to Grow,* you may wonder why this title was chosen. There may be a question in your mind, such as, why write another book on church growth? This is a legitimate question as there have been hundreds of books written on the subject of church growth in the past 40 years. It would seem that this topic would have been exhausted by now. Then, why should I write another book on this subject? Most books on this subject explain these principles quite clearly, but what I believe is lacking are practical models showing how to apply these principles to grow churches.

Another reason for writing this book is to convince pastors that you do not have to be a superpreacher to grow a church. This idea is preeminent throughout this discourse.

I will share an incident which occurred in my first pastoral assignment that had an impact on my style of preaching. On this particular Sunday, I had decided to change my mode of preaching to more of a style of getting the congregation fired up. After the worship service each Sunday as we traveled the 100 miles back home, my wife, Shirley, would critique my sermon. During that time, I noticed there seemed to be a change in my wife's demeanor. Her evaluation of my sermon consisted of just five words: "Have you lost your mind?" It is not my intention to make any value judgment of any preaching style, but it was obvious that that particular style was not a natural fit for me.

It is my intent to show how these principles enable churches to participate more effectively in implementing Jesus' mandate to "go and make disciples of all nations." First, let us understand what a church growth principle is. "A church growth principle is a universal truth, which, when properly interpreted and applied, contributes significantly to the growth of churches."

God and Numbers

First, I would like to dispel the myth that church growth is only concerned with numbers. Practitioners of the church growth movement are frequently criticized for playing the numbers game. Church growth proponents are often accused of overemphasizing quantity to the neglect of quality.

Unfortunately, the word "growth" causes many people to think only in terms of numbers. How often have we heard church members make such statements as, "We are more interested in spirituality than numbers." There is nothing inherently wrong with numbers, although it should not be the primary reason for bringing members into the church. There are many ways to bring members into the church, and many of these methods have little to do with making disciples. Then our real concern should be how the numbers are obtained.

It appears that many churches today focus more on entertainment, and many of them are good at it. We have not always put enough emphasis on making disciples, and this requires teaching. There is nothing unholy about numbers in themselves. God must have been interested in numbers because he named a book in the Old Testament "Numbers." It is reasonable to assume that a church with 30 members can be just as unholy or unspiritual as a church with thousands of members.

When we consider models of church growth, we usually think of churches throughout the country whose numbers have swelled to tens of thousands in their congregations. However, it is a fact that every church is not destined to be a mega-church. It is erroneous to assume that church growth is just a numbers game. The term "church growth" invokes a variety of attitudes, emotions, and responses. Such attitudes usually preclude the possibility of any numerical increase in churches. It is interesting to note that pastors that have large memberships never complain that they have too many members. On the other hand, most negative comments usually come from those who have only a few members.

George Barna, a church researcher, states that the average Protestant congregation in America has 50 to 60 adults who regularly attend Sunday morning worship services. I have observed that churches usually grow to a certain point and then level off in attendance at some point, where the membership may range in the following brackets: –5, 70–85, 115–135, 175–250, etc

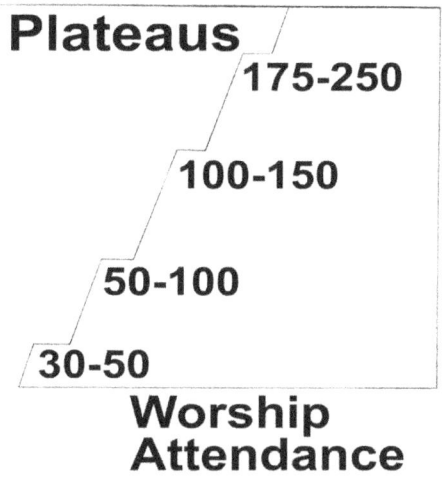

In order to move from one plateau to another, a church must begin thinking, acting, witnessing, and serving like a church on the next plateau. As an example, a church of 35 members must begin doing things like a church of 75 members. Therefore, the focus of this book is churches with fewer than 250 members. So, how large should a church become? Is it reaching its potential of growth in the community it serves? (Even though I am certified as a church growth consultant, I often use the term "church potential" instead of church growth.) Is the church taking advantage of the opportunities for ministry? Has it found its niche? The answer is quite simple. Every church should have enough members to create and maintain ministries which meet needs of those living in the community it serves.

The principles and strategies discussed herein come as a result of workshops, seminars, conferences, and real-life experiences. There are certain principles at work in situations where churches are growing. When a church ceases to grow, it is a reflection of the attitudes of both the members and pastor. Churches can grow if certain conditions are met. It can grow if: (1) It is a healthy congregation; (2) It is willing to invest in growth; (3) It makes use of church growth principles; (4) It has a passion to reach the unsaved. This is evidenced in hundreds of congregations throughout the country which are experiencing growth. Healthy churches grow. It follows that if the church is unhealthy, it does not grow.

GEOMETRIC MODEL FOR CHURCH GROWTH
EQUILATERAL TRIANGLE

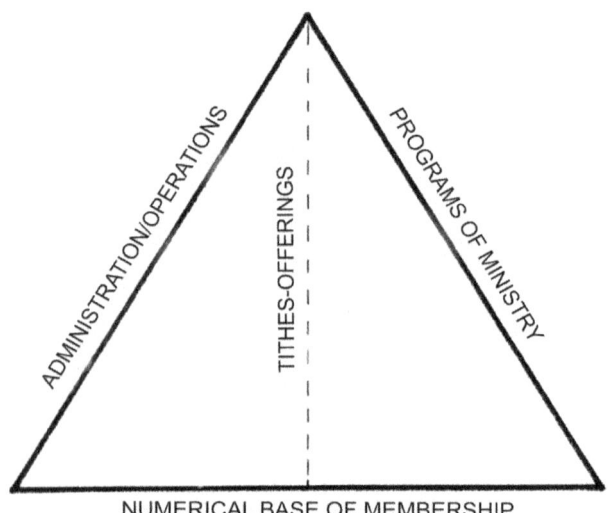

This figure represents the balance between three factors which determine a healthy state of growth in the church.

The altitude of the triangle represents the church's income in the form of tithes and offerings, which supports the costs of operations, administration, and programs of ministry.

As the administrative level rises, there is a corresponding increase in programs of ministry offered. It is necessary that we increase the base of membership in order that the symmetry of the figure may be maintained.

In observing congregations and denominations that have lost large numbers of members in the past 30 or 40 years, church growth experts find that it is difficult to turn this process around, even though we know those things which make for growth. The problem in this area is not unlike the problems in other areas of our lives; knowing and doing something about it are not the same. Therefore, the problem lies with each of us. If our churches are to grow, we will have to change our mind-set.

Jesus left us a mandate to "Go," but too often, we just wait for people to "come." We only have to look at the phenomenal growth of the church recorded in the book of Acts to see the truth behind this mandate. Jesus and the disciples "went" to wherever the people were.

Our faith requires more than just institutional maintenance. It demands that we become disciples and witness to the lost souls in our communities.

Before we proceed further, I think it is necessary that we take a look at how the church grew in the book of Acts.

Growth in the Book of Acts

God is interested in numbers. This is implied in the Great Commission as stated in Matthew 28:19–20, where the Lord commands us to "Go therefore and make disciples of all nations…"

The book of Acts recorded the phenomenal growth of the New Testament church by quoting numbers.

Acts 2:41: Then those who gladly received his word were baptized on that day and about ***3,000 souls*** were added to the church on the day of Pentecost.

Acts 2:47: And the Lord added to the church daily, such as should be saved.

Acts 4:4: Howbeit, many of them that heard believed and the numbers of the men were ***about 5,000.***

Acts 6:7: And the work of God increased; and the number of the disciples ***multiplied*** in Jerusalem greatly.

Acts 21:20: And when they heard it, they glorified the Lord, and saith unto him, Thou seeth, brother, how ***many thousands*** of Jews here are which believe, and they are zealous of the law.

God's will for Christians today is clear. He wants his church to grow spiritually and numerically. The same Holy Spirit who filled believers and sent them preaching the gospel on Pentecost is available to us today. The harvest is out there waiting to be told the Good News and become faithful disciples. God wants your church to grow.

There is a positive relationship between church growth and church health, and this relationship is represented by numbers. Healthy churches attract people; unhealthy churches do not. Church growth relates to the number of new members, number of baptisms, and the number of ministries. Church health is related to how well the body of Christ functions in terms of fulfilling God's mission and purpose. Healthy churches are more effective when the six purposes in the book of Acts 2:42–

47 are intentional, active, and balanced. These purposes are: (1) Fellowship (2) Worship (3) Ministry (4) Discipleship (5) Evangelism, and (6) Prayer.

This book is more than just to be read. It is designed as a guide or a tool to be used by congregations to become more effective in fulfilling the mandate which Jesus stated in Matthew 28:19–20. It is essential that as many members as possible participate in an organized study of this book. If these principles of growth are diligently applied, your church will grow. This process must include the pastor, officers, Sunday School teachers, and other significant persons and groups. This book is not intended as an academic endeavor, but it does present ideas and methods that can be used by pastors and laypersons to increase membership in their churches.

EXERCISE

Healthy churches are more effective when the six purposes in the book of Acts (2:42–47) are intentional, active, and in balance. These purposes are:

1. _____

2. _____

3. _____

4. _____

5. _____

6. _____

Chapter 1

CONDITIONS FOR CHURCH GROWTH

"Go, therefore and make disciples of all nations ..."

A healthy church is one that has a well-defined mission and purpose that is communicated and understood by its members. Even though it has many members and organizations, they all function as one body striving toward the same goal, focusing on the biblical mission and purpose for the church's existence.

A healthy church is likened unto the human body: It must have regular checkups to assess how well it is doing and how well all systems are functioning. If any part is not functioning properly and is not corrected quickly, that problem can weaken or prohibit the proper functioning of other systems, thereby causing the body to malfunction or become diseased.

A church that is healthy is one that reevaluates itself and makes adjustments when necessary in order to keep the church body well and able to function at its optimum potential, which lines up with its purpose and with the scripture.

A healthy church is one where its body understands Christ's mandate of making disciples. Thus, all its efforts, services, programs, and outreaches are geared to that end—making disciples for Christ.

Principle #2: Churches grow when evangelism is one of the highest priorities of ministry

Churches grow when growth principles are utilized as the basis of understanding the process of growing the church. The first consideration is to understand what a church growth principle is. Let me reiterate. "A church growth principle is a universal truth, which, when properly interpreted and applied, contributes significantly to the growth of churches."

Church Health

Several analogies used of the church in the New Testament concern the Body of Christ. "For as the body is one, and has many members, and all the members of that one body, being many, are one body: so also is Christ" (I Corinthians 12:12–26). "For as in one body we have many members, and all the members do not have the same function, so we, though we are many, are one body in Christ …" (Romans 12:4).

The church is a live organism, and live organisms are predisposed to diseases and illnesses. The church, as the body of Christ, must be healthy in order to grow. When an organism contracts a disease, its health is affected. Just as our physical body can catch various diseases, so can the body of Christ. In other words, the organism becomes ill, and sometimes the illness is terminal.

Sick churches, like sick people, do not grow very well. On the other hand, if the sickness is diagnosed and treated in time, most illnesses can be cured and growth can again happen. Let us look at several factors which help church growth.

GEOMETRIC MODEL FOR CHURCH GROWTH
ISOSCELES TRIANGLE

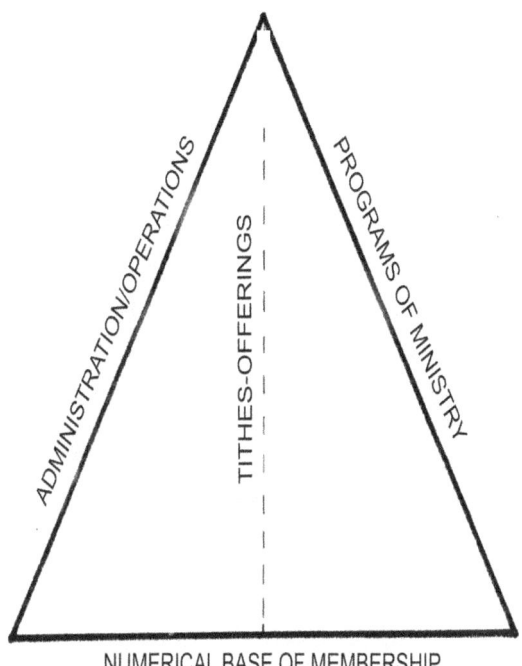

In this figure, the sides have been increased in length without a corresponding increase in the base.

This results in a smaller base of membership supporting increasing costs of administration and operations, along with increasing ministries of the church.

The base of membership must be increased in order to support the rising costs of operations and programs of ministry.

How effective the church implements the mandate when Jesus commissioned the disciples in Matthew 28:19–20 depends on three factors:

Investing Resources in Growth

God has placed both financial and human resources in congregations. The leadership of the church should provide the opportunity for the members to use their gifts and talents in the church.

Making Use of Church Growth Principles

We are aware of the decline of many mainline denominations and churches today, but we have not addressed the problem. There are biblical growth principles that can reverse this problem of declining congregations. Realizing that there are many growth principles, I have chosen ten basic principles drawn from my experience as a pastor and a church consultant.

Have a Passion to Reach the Unsaved

We must recognize that people without Jesus are really lost and the only way people can come to Jesus is by our witness that Jesus Christ is our Savior and Lord. Christians must take seriously the mandate that Jesus left us when he called us to go and make disciples. Scripture is clear that God wants all men to be saved. Christians must have an unwavering passion to fulfill that mandate.

On many occasions, I have asked church members if they would like to see their church grow. The results of this unofficial polling indicate that more than 90 percent of the people answered "yes" to this question. Yes, they verbalized that they desired their church to grow, but they were not willing to apply growth principles, methods, and techniques which would ensure growth.

Like anything worthwhile, there is a cost factor attached, the same for growing a church. Often members are not willing to pay the cost of bringing new members into the church. Church growth is not an easy way out because it entails hard work. If we desire our church to grow, we will have to count the cost. Jesus addressed this when he said, "for which of you, intending to build a tower, who did not first sit down and count the cost..." (Luke 14:28). The cost will include time, energy, and money. The financial cost isn't the greatest barrier to growth. It will cost a change in attitudes, and this is the greatest barrier to overcome. Symbolically, and also realistically, you must "Be willing to give up your seat." You have to make room in your heart to accept new people who may have new ideas, people who may not dress like you, look like you, or even talk like you.

This book will highlight ten universal growth principles that can be utilized by pastors to stimulate growth in their churches. Throughout this book you will see how one or more of these principles are being utilized. Perhaps these growth principles should be listed before we go further.

What is a Church Growth Principle?

A church growth principle is a universal truth when properly interpreted and applied, contributes significantly to the growth of churches.

1. **Churches grow when there is a strong commitment to discipleship.**

2. **Churches grow when evangelism is one of the highest priorities of ministry.**
   Reaching the unsaved is the mandate which Jesus left for believers in Matthew 28.

3. **Orderliness: churches grow when the facility is attractive with clean restrooms.**
   This is one principle which is consistent with all growing churches. When the facility is kept clean and attractive, people feel that this is carried over in the total administrative organization of the church. Adequate parking and seating in the sanctuary is also necessary. When the sanctuary is 80 percent full, another service should be started. If the parking lot is filled to capacity, people will continue on to another church where there is adequate parking.

4. **The leadership strength of the pastor and favorable transition of pastors is a prime factor in growing a church.**
   A Christian leader must be called by God to lead and must possess Christian character. He\she must be able to influence those who he/she is called to lead.

5. **Organizing small groups and delegating leadership enhances church growth.**
   Churches grow as they are offered a variety of choices of

ministry. Organizing small groups addresses the varied interests and needs of the members.

6. **Growth occurs when marketing techniques are utilized.** Church marketing is the performance of both business and ministry activities that impact the church's target audience with the intention of ministering to and fulfilling their spiritual, social, emotional, and physical needs and thereby satisfy the ministry goals of the church.

7. **Churches grow as they participate in the social arena and make good relationships with city officials and local residents (social ministries, block parties, etc.).** Many churches are fulfilling the social mandate by involvement in both social service and social action on behalf of the poor. "The spirit of the Lord is upon me, because he has anointed me to preach the gospel to the poor; he has sent me to heal the brokenhearted, to preach deliverance to the captives, recovering of sight to the blind, to set at liberty them that are bruised, to preach the acceptable year of the Lord" (Luke 4:18–19).

8. **Churches grow when worship is done with excellence.** Dynamic worship is an important factor for determining the health of a congregation.

9. **Friendliness of the congregation assures growth** When visitors arrive at the parking lot, they should be greeted immediately and escorted to the entrance of the church. They should be accompanied by someone from

the time they enter the church parking lot until the time of the benediction closing the worship service.

10. Spiritual gifts enhance church growth
Every born-again Christian has been given at least one spiritual gift. These gifts are given for the edification of the body of Christ and must be encouraged.

Churches will reach their potential when members are willing to apply church growth principles. A great number of growing churches in the United States are intentionally using these principles and are experiencing growth. At the same time, many churches and denominations are in a state of decline because of their reluctance to use church growth principles. These principles are adaptable to both large and small churches. Do not lose heart, because every large church was at one time a small church.

The church is usually referred to as a living organism. This implies that it is alive. Living organisms can be infected by different kinds of diseases, and some of these diseases are terminal. An excellent tool used to determine the health of a church is the Church Growth Diagnostic Clinic, by the Charles E. Fuller Institute of Evangelism & Church Growth. Old age is diagnosed as an aging congregation that dies off because it never replaces lost members or embraces new ideas. A symptom of this disease is a growing percentage of members are over 50. Old age tends to set in when there is an out-migration of people from the community, or there is a change in the ethnic population. Unless there is some type of intervening event which changes this condition, it becomes terminal.

Church growth thinking was given a great thrust with the establishment of the Institute of Church Growth in Eugene, Oregon, approximately 50 years ago. The institute was later moved to Fuller Seminary, and it became a full-fledged graduate school and the Fuller Evangelistic Association, a department of church growth. As a result of these events, students from all walks of life entered Fuller to study church growth principles, techniques, and methods. Many of these students went on to establish mega-churches throughout the United States. This was a new phenomenon on the American scene.

As the movement developed, it seems that it lost its primary focus of making disciples. The mega-church is able to take the worship experience to a different level, sometimes resembling a well orchestrated production. It seems today that people respond to large crowds as if to imply that "Bigger is better." Many persons that I have talked to who attend mega-churches usually say, "I attend ..." instead of saying, "I belong to ..." a certain church. Could it be that they are just consumers instead of participants in the ministry of the church? I think that there is common agreement that worship is the primary building block of our faith. This is well and good, but if our experience as a Christian ends with just the worship experience, we have not received all that God has for us.

Christians understand that Jesus mandated that we go and make disciples of all nations. Sometime ago, I was browsing in a Christian bookstore and noticed a book by Walter A. Henrichsen with the title *Disciples Are Made Not Born*. Just the title of this book reinforced my position that it is necessary for members to receive a significant amount of training to become a disciple. The question is, how do we "go and make disciples" in this society, which is quite different today and is still in a state of continuous change? My intention for writing this book, *Ten Church Growth Principles,* is to show how these principles enable churches to participate more effectively in implementing Jesus' mandate to "go and make disciples of all nations." The following information regarding Rev. T. P. Lee is a prime example of the principle on commitment.

Reverend T. P. Lee

Reverend T. P. Lee, a pastor of a small congregation in the high desert, had invited me to visit the church where he was the founding pastor. Pop Lee, as he was affectionately called, was held in the highest esteem by all who had the good fortune of knowing him. It was a cold, rainy day in the month of February when we arrived at the small town of Victorville, California. We noticed a sign on the freeway that indicated the population to be 14,000 inhabitants. This pastor had predicted three years previously that I would be called to preach.

This was a most intriguing experience as we traveled through a mountain pass to the summit at an elevation of nearly 5,000 feet. This is known as the Cajon Pass. Before us was a panoramic view of a vast area that is known as the "high desert." The scene before us was not picturesque by any stretch of the imagination. There was one feature which was rather prominent throughout the landscape. It really appeared to be out of place in this barren

CONDITIONS FOR CHURCH GROWTH

landscape because of its appearance. This specimen was not one of nature's finest offerings of beauty. Later, I learned that this grotesque creation was called a "Joshua tree," and it was a protected species. I certainly would agree why such a specimen would have to be protected.

Within a short time we were in the town of Victorville on E Street. We observed several churches as we proceeded along E Street before arriving at our destination, which was Emmanuel Temple Church, housed in a small, unattractive, run-down building. We opened our umbrellas to shield ourselves from the rain as we walked hurriedly to the entrance of the church.

As we entered the building, we were utterly amazed to see that a number of the members also had open umbrellas protecting themselves from the rain that was leaking profusely through the roof of the building. I had never witnessed a scene like this before. Now, there is nothing unusual about people assembling on a Sunday morning to worship God, but there was something different about this gathering. This was certainly a display of commitment and dedication on the part of the pastor and members of this congregation.

The faith and dedication of Pastor Lee and these few members had kept this congregation together 23 years, overcoming many difficulties and challenges. They had even experienced a short period of "homelessness" on one occasion. As we fast-forward to 25 years later, we see that this small congregation has grown to more than 2,000 members. The question is, what were the intervening events which brought about this increase in membership?

My Growing Up Years

Growing up in my family was a wonderful experience. We received lots of love and support. As we discussed the various issues affecting our community, we were taught to defend our ideas and positions on the many issues we discussed around the table at dinnertime. Yes, we also discussed biblical principles and issues. Many of our values were taught and reinforced in daily discussions around the dinner table. This was an experience that the whole family enjoyed and looked forward to each day.

My young adult years were spent completing my college degree and doing a three-year tour in the army. During the time in service, I usually managed to attend worship services when I had weekend leave. Members of the churches that we visited would usually show their appreciation for the sacrifice we were making to protect our country. This appreciation was often shown by inviting us into their homes for dinner. I must confess that our motivation to attend church was not always primarily to worship.

We were aware that many of the members of the congregations had young adult children, and many of them were of the opposite sex. These young ladies also felt that it was their patriotic duty to entertain us. Their patriotic commitment made such an impression on us that we usually arranged our schedules to accommodate them. However, on a more serious note, my attending church while I was in the army was the result of the values instilled in me in my formative years. The habit of attending church was just a natural thing to do.

My tour of duty was during the Korean conflict. After completing Basic Training and Leadership School, I was assigned to Headquarters European Command. Eventually my duty assignment was with a newly formed "Bastard Outfit," teaching nonmilitary subjects. This unit was unique in that it wasn't standard army organization. It became known as the 7744 Educational Training Unit. This duty assignment turned out to be quite exciting as I really enjoyed teaching. In fact, I began to consider teaching after returning to the States. Little did I realize at this time that God was preparing me for future endeavors.

The thought of becoming a teacher became more predominant in my thinking. After being discharged from the army, I enrolled in classes which were required for a teaching credential in the state of California. What about the vow I made concerning not to become a teacher? Well, I made another vow: "Never Say Never." As I look in retrospect at these events, I am convinced that there are no accidents in God's economy. Every experience has meaning and purpose in our lives. God does order our steps. These experiences proved to be of great value in the pastoral ministry.

In 1955, my father passed away after a lengthy illness. He had been one of my greatest encouragers and supporters. It seemed as if it was the providence of God that he lived to see me accomplish many of my goals. At the same time, I had passed all parts of the teacher examination, which was required by the Los Angeles Unified School District. I was offered a contract, which I signed, and was hired as a teacher immediately.

At this point, I embarked upon a career of 29 years in education. One particular highlight of my tenure of teaching was being awarded grants on two occasions for innovative teaching of math and science.

During my tenure in the Los Angeles City School District, I served as a teacher, math coordinator, mental health counselor, and a master teacher, training prospective teachers from the University of Southern California.

Further in this book I will describe how these experiences were a period of preparation for my future calling to the ministry. There is no doubt in my mind that God prepares us for any endeavor or purpose in our lives. St. Paul's life is a prime example of this principle. He was a citizen of Rome as he was born in Tarsus, a city in the Roman province of Cilicia. This granted him certain privileges other Jewish persons did not enjoy. He was reared under Greek influences of philosophy. At the age of 13, he was sent to Jerusalem to study the scriptures under Gamaliel, the most prominent rabbi of the day. He was a member of the distinguished tribe of Benjamin and a Pharisee; he was also a member of the Sanhedrin, the highest governing body of the Jews. We can readily see how his life experiences prepared him for spreading this young, struggling Christian faith.

In the formative years of my life, I made two vows which I struggled to keep. I vowed that I would never become a preacher or teacher. There were real practical reasons why these vows were made. The number-one reason was that most of my immediate and extended family were either preachers or teachers. Therefore, I came to the conclusion that there must be other options to consider as a career.

The other situation that influenced my decision not to become a preacher was the itinerate ministry. When one enters the pastoral ministry of the Methodist Church, he/she takes a vow to accept being assigned as pastor to churches by the presiding bishop. Sometimes there is some discrepancy regarding the principle of itinerancy and how it is practiced.

My father was a teacher and school administrator when God called him to be a preacher. The first few years of his ministry were bivocational: teaching and pastoring. He eventually resigned his administrative position as a school principal and entered the itinerant ministry on a full-time basis. Becoming a traveling elder required accepting assignments to other churches at the discretion of the presiding bishop.

During the next five years, he was assigned to five different churches. During the period of my elementary education, I attended five elementary schools in different towns and cities. My brothers, sisters, and I didn't perceive these moves as being too difficult to adjust to. Actually, we found this annual event to be quite exciting as we looked forward to meeting new friends and traveling to a new town. Of course, as we matured, we began to understand why my mother's perception of this experience was radically different from ours. With each approaching annual conference, it appeared that my mother's demeanor would undergo a definite change. It ultimately became clear to us that she was experiencing feelings of fear, anxiety, even resentment.

I can remember quite vividly those occasions when the bishop ascended to that position of prominence behind the pulpit to read the pastoral appointments. The audience would sit there in a tense state of anticipation as they witnessed the bishop rising to read the appointments. The bishop would begin by informing the congregation that assigning pastors to churches was an awesome responsibility as he had agonized through hours of prayer seeking God's "godly judgment" concerning this matter. Because of witnessing these annual proceedings for several years, I began to experience some difficulty reconciling whether the bishop's "godly judgment" was always "godly" when he made certain pastoral appointments.

CONDITIONS FOR CHURCH GROWTH

EXERCISE

1. A healthy church is one that has a well-defined _____ _____ and is understood by the _____ of the church.

2. "… for which of you, intending to build a tower, sitteth not down first, and counteth the costs, whether he have sufficiency to finish it?" What must be considered before starting any program or project?
   (1) _____
   (2) _____
   (3) _____

3. List three factors which will ensure the growth of your church.
   (1) _____
   (2) _____
   (3) _____

Chapter 2

EVANGELISM

The church is usually referred to as the Body of Christ; therefore, it is natural for it to grow and reproduce itself. This is true only when the church is healthy. Evangelism is the process through which people become disciples of Christ and responsible members of the church. Churches that are obedient to the mandate make it a high priority. ("Go therefore and make disciples of all nations, baptizing them in the name of the Father, the Son, and the Holy Spirit, teaching them to observer all that I have commanded you; and lo, I am with you always, even to the end of the age.") Too often, this mandate is not the highest priority in many churches today. It seems as if many churches are just doing business as usual. However, the mandate has not changed during these 2,000 years after Jesus spoke these words; it is the same yesterday, today, and forever. What has changed are the methods and techniques used to grow churches today.

Many evangelistic methods today are not as effective as they were in the past. One method which has been used extensively is canvassing neighborhoods by "knocking on doors." Research shows that this method of evangelism reaches only one person out of 100 contacts (1 percent). This is statistically true, but there are two exceptions to this rule; namely, the Church of the Latter Day Saints and Jehovah's Witnesses. These two institutions saturate communities with such massive numbers it would appear that their returns are much greater than 1 percent. It becomes obvious that one of the factors in the equation changes. It is quite simple to get larger numbers of commitment just by sending greater numbers of people into the community who have undergone extensive training. The ratio of contacts vs. commitments remains 100 to 1.

It is not my intent to imply that the door-to-door canvassing should not be practiced. There are occasions when it is advantageous to participate in this activity. Yet, there are other methods of reaching the lost or unchurched in which the returns are far greater than the practice of door-to-door canvassing.

During my years of serving as a pastor and consulting with local churches and several denominations, I have arrived at certain conclusions regarding churches' attitudes regarding evangelism and church growth. Apparently evangelism does not occupy a position of high priority in many churches, and even in some denominations, for that matter.

Many professing Christians today have not undergone training in discipleship even though Jesus instructs us to make disciples. It is no wonder that so many Christians aren't proficient in sharing their faith effectively. They may be somewhat insecure to do so. This is not to imply that they are not committed or lacking in faith. It is likely that they have not been taught how to effectively share their faith with the unchurched. Often when asked, "Why are you a Christian?" or why they are a member of a church, their answer is somewhat vague and does not convey a clear understanding of their faith. Members are usually zealous about their faith but aren't able to communicate it effectively. Could it be that churches have not always followed the mandate to make disciples as stated by Jesus in the Gospel of Matthew?

Most evangelism efforts today focus on "making decisions" to accept Christ as Savior and Lord. *Evangelism* is an outreach tool used to bring the unchurched to church, whereas, *Discipleship* is the process of teaching those who have made a decision to become a mature Christian. The new convert will grow through the knowledge and understanding of the faith. Evangelism is the tool or method through which a person is introduced to Christ. This is often done by sharing a personal experience with a friend or relative. This method is usually referred to as "Relational Evangelism." This is the most effective method of sharing the faith.

Sharing Christ can be done not only through a personal testimony, but also by using various tracts designed for this purpose. If there is no follow-up after the brief commitment, it is questionable whether this person has become a disciple of Christ at this point. Becoming a disciple requires teaching. Being a disciple of Christ means reaching non-Christians, and then teaching them how to grow spiritually and how to make more new disciples. This process of learning to become a disciple requires hours of study.

Discipleship Programs

There are four discipleship programs of which I am familiar, and I have successfully used two of them. They are (1) Rick Warren's Four Covenating Classes, (2) *The Master's Plan For Making Disciples*, by Win & Charles Arn, (3) *Evangelism Explosion*, by James Kennedy, (4) *The Cleansing Stream*, by Jack Hayford. Each of these plans offers a unique approach in teaching discipleship.

These programs of ministry are based on New Testament strategies of sharing God's love that goes beyond "making decisions." They share a common objective, which is making disciples and responsible church members. Each of these discipleship programs teaches members how to spend time with God, emphasizes prayer, teaches tithing, and develops fellowship among members. As a pastor, I have always required new members to attend orientation classes, which are Discipleship 101 and Discipleship 201, before receiving them as full-fledged members of the church.

We have experienced phenomenal results in using the Cleansing Stream program. Over a period of nine years, 700 people have successfully completed the program. Many of these believers have experienced a new level of freedom, maturity, and commitment. The four areas of concentration are:

Session one:	Alignment ... Calls us to walk in the spirit
Session two:	Consecration ... Causes us to commit everything to Jesus
Session three:	Words ... Calls us to speak words of life

Session four: Calls us to enter the Cleansing Stream and experience God's ongoing freedom and restoration

The objective of being "Cleansed For The Master's Use" has provided a focus, and then the end goal for each person. A key goal for a participant in the seminar is to experience the freedom in Christ that frees them to move in ministry for Christ in a more effective way. Many of our participants completed the seminar and moved into ministry or became more effective in the ministries they have worked in prior to the seminar. This seminar has changed lives and with that change has come the desire and heart to serve God and his people through the body of Christ—the church.

Varieties of New Persons Joining Churches

People joining by transfer do not contribute to the building of the kingdom. When people join by transfer from another church, they are merely changing their membership from one location to another location. Years ago at parties, children would play the game of "Musical Chairs." Today, this game is played out in churches as "Musical Pews."

New converts are vitally important to a healthy growing church. In order to build the kingdom of God, we must reach the vast number of unsaved or unchurched people in every community in America. Research shows that 70 percent of people in any community in America are either unsaved or unchurched (Barna). Jesus said to the 70 disciples as he sent them out to witness, "… The harvest truly is great, but the laborers are few…" (Luke 10:2).

New Members

Often people attending the worship service are overwhelmed by the music of the choir and the inspiring and dynamic preaching of the pastor. They then anxiously await the opportunity to walk forward when the pastor declares, "The doors of the church are open." As they come forward to unite with the church, too often they are not informed that it is required that they attend orientation and discipleship classes. On many occasions, I have observed that they are surprised when they are informed that to be granted full membership there is a requirement to complete certain orientation classes. This is an essential component in the assimilation process, however.

When individuals unite with the church, they must be required to make a commitment to attend the New Member Orientation class, which is Discipleship 101. Discipleship 201 deals with growing in spiritual maturity, which is a discipleship program written by Rick Warren. This process is effective as the first steps in assimilating new members into the church. This is also the first step in fulfilling the mandate that Jesus made in Matthew 28:19-20 concerning making disciples.

We are commissioned to go and witness today just as the 70 were commissioned by Jesus to go. This means taking advantage of every opportunity to share the Good News by witnessing to the saving power of Jesus Christ. I am pleased to see that so many churches are laying hold of the vision and taking advantage of the opportunity for making disciples.

God has blessed many churches with the necessary resources to do the work of winning souls to Christ. The question remains, "How can the church respond to the opportunity to witness to the lost souls in communities today?" We must do evangelism differently in a society which is in constant change. We must be more innovative and creative in our strategies and methods in this postmodern culture today.

It is my intent to present and explain workable principles, practices, and insights in this book to assist pastors in producing both quantitative and qualitative growth in their churches. This is the process of fulfilling the mandate of making disciples. "Go ye therefore and teach all nations, baptizing them in the name of the Father, the Son, and the Holy Ghost: teaching them to observe all things whatsoever I have commanded you: and lo, I am with you always, even unto the end of the world" (Matthew 28:19-20). All is for the glory of God. It is often stated that evangelism is the life blood of the church.

We have established that the church is a living organism, and like other organisms, it is sometimes infected with disease. There is a disease of the blood called anemia, sometimes referred to as "Tired Blood." When this happens, the blood is weak and unable to carry the vital life-sustaining qualities to sustain life. If evangelism is not seen as a high priority, if it isn't organized effectively, if it isn't funded properly, if it isn't making disciples, it has now contracted the disease of anemia. This is sometimes a terminal disease.

Evangelism is the process through which people develop a relationship with Jesus Christ. Traditionally, evangelism has focused primarily on making decisions for Christ. The evangelism committee usually teaches members how to use the spiritual laws, then sends them out to witness. The contacts are given tracts and repeat the sinner's prayer. They then are told that they are now saved. This does have some value, but it is just the beginning of the new Christian's journey of becoming a disciple of Christ. The new convert must be "discipled," and this requires a considerable amount of training. Every Christian is mandated to witness to the Good News of Jesus Christ, not just the pastor or the evangelism committee. It follows that every activity the church engages in must be based on and related to the mandate which Jesus stated in the Gospel of Matthew.

Church growth is a science. Viewed as such, leaders can investigate the nature, function, and health of churches as they relate to the effective implementation of the Great Commission. Church growth requires three essential factors: measurement, research, and evaluation. It is not just a theory; it is a practical approach in putting into practice the Great Commission.

In our contemporary society, it is essential that we look at facts and other data to measure results. The primary question that must be asked is, is the church growing, or is it in decline? If the church is in decline, it should enter into a process of diagnosis to determine the reasons why it finds itself in a declining mode.

On many occasions throughout the course of my consulting career, I have used an effective tool to determine the health of a church developed by the Church Growth Diagnostic Clinic at the Charles E. Fuller Institute of Evangelism & Church Growth. This clinic points out the vital signs of a healthy church, and it also exposes some of the common factors of declining churches. It presents guidelines for analyzing and diagnosing the problems designed to assist local churches with understanding their growth trends, evaluate their programs, and measure their volunteer involvement and potential for ministry in their community. It is a personalized, comprehensive model. This tool may be modified to make it applicable to specific conditions of different churches.

Renewal of Established Churches

Evangelism usually is not a priority in many established churches. It seems that in established churches, much energy is expended in taking care of in-house business instead of focusing on those outside of the church. Research indicates that 70 percent of people in any community are unsaved or unchurched. Jesus states, "… the harvest is truly great, but the laborers are few: pray ye therefore the Lord of the harvest, that he would send forth laborers into his harvest" (Luke 10:2).

When a new pastor is assigned or called to an established church, he has not earned credibility or respect as a leader at this point. It usually takes three or four years to be accepted as the leader of the congregation. After about three years, pastors can exercise greater influence in their church and are able to implement their vision. This is why a short pastoral tenure is not conducive to church growth. When members join the church, they are usually "joining the pastor." The very idea of members joining the pastor is not always looked upon in a positive way by some pastors, denominational officials, and members of established churches, however.

My background of experience convinces me that it is more difficult to renew an established or traditional church than it is to start a new church. Renewing a traditional church presents serious challenges, but it can be done. Lyle Schaller, a prominent church consultant, states that "It's a mistake to attempt to revitalize existing congregations at the expense of church planting." Why is Schaller correct in his statement? The changes which have taken place in our society have created a considerable impact on the Christian community. Younger persons seemingly have freed themselves from the traditional views of the Christian church. They live by a different group of values, they communicate differently, and they even have a different worldview. These young people have been categorized as Generation X, and only 15 percent of these persons attend church regularly. Pastors must present Christ to the world as it is—not as it was or as we would like it to be. To reach this group, the church must communicate the gospel in a manner that is relevant to it.

Resistance to Change

The primary reason why it is difficult to renew a traditional church is because traditional members are extremely resistant to change. Over a period of years, established churches have developed their own traditions which were relevant in the past. Chances are we are all familiar with an old adage which states, "The sands of time are littered with the bones of institutions which refused to change." I think it's important that that we explore some of these reasons why people resist change.

First, people resist change because of *misunderstandings.* When people do not understand why they should change, they will work very hard to oppose it. It is important that the pastor take the necessary time to explain how the changes will benefit the congregation.

Second, people resist change because *there is a cost,* and members usually are not willing to pay the price for change. Sometimes the reward for change is too small for their effort; therefore, they are not willing to pay the price.

Third, people are uncomfortable in *getting out of old habit patterns.* They offer resistance when they feel that they have to do something differently from the way that they are used to doing things.

Fourth, people oppose change because of *lack of ownership.* When church members are not involved in the change process, they resist anything that they feel is being pushed upon them. In planning the process of vision, the pastor must involve key leaders of the church.

Fifth, people resist change when they are *threatened with the loss of something that is valuable* to them. People resist change most when they feel that they are losing security, money, or control.

Sixth, another reason people resist change is a *negative attitude toward change in general.* Some people's entire thought process is based on the idea that nothing should ever be changed.

Seventh, *tradition* is the last reason why people fight change. The attitude is usually expressed in this manner: "We've never done it that way before."

EVANGELISM

Relational Evangelism

Win Arm, of the Institute of American Church Growth, conducted a survey to determine how people come into the church. Fourteen thousand laypersons were asked the question, "Who was responsible for your coming to Christ and to your church?" One of the following eight responses was given. The results of this study indicate that 85 percent of people who visit the church are invited by friends or neighbors.

1. Some said a "special need" brought them to Christ and the church
2. Some responded they just "walked in"
3. Some listed the "pastor"
4. Some indicated "visitation"
5. Some mentioned the "Sunday School"
6. Some listed "evangelistic crusade" or television show (revival)
7. Some recalled that the church "program" attracted them
8. Some responded that a "friend or relative" was the reason they are now in Christ or in church

Here are the results.

Special need	2%
Walk-in	1%
Pastor	5%
Visitation	1%
Sunday School	5%
Program	2%
Evangelistic Crusade (Revival)	.05%
Friends and Relatives	85%

The results of this survey indicate that the most effective strategy of evangelism is the result of members becoming proficient in sharing their faith with friends, neighbors, and relatives. This is usually referred to as Relational Evangelism. People share best with those that they know best. Therefore, any evangelistic effort should concentrate on teaching members how to effectively share their faith with their circle of friends and neighbors. Most people have an average of eight intimate friends. Among these eight intimate friends a number of them are likely to be unchurched or unsaved.

The Amos Temple Model

One classic example of Relational Evangelism was demonstrated during my tenure as pastor at Amos Temple Church in Riverside, California. Marge was a faithful member who was actively involved in several ministries at Amos Temple. I noticed that each Sunday as visitors were recognized in the worship service, two or three of these visitors would simply say, "We came to visit this church because Marge sent us." This event would occur on a consistent basis, and I became curious as to why this was happening.

Eventually a conference was arranged with Marge. I asked Marge how she was able to invite so many people to worship at Amos Temple. She informed me that she was the proprietor of a beauty salon, and she would always talk about her church and invite her customers to come and worship at her church. Marge talked about her church with such enthusiasm and excitement.

Many of her customers apparently shared in this excitement and decided to come and see for themselves what was happening at her church. I'm not aware whether Marge ever used a tract in her relationship with her many friends and acquaintances in inviting them to her church. One thing is apparent, however; she was evangelizing according to a New Testament plan of church growth.

Let me share a passage of scripture that illustrates an effective witness about Andrew, Simon Peter's brother. *"He first findeth his own brother Simon,* and saith unto him, we have found the Messiah, which is, being interpreted the Christ. And *he brought him to Jesus ..."* (John 1:40–42). Marge was functioning as an Andrew by sending and bringing people to church. More Andrews are needed to witness boldly to the saving power of Jesus Christ.

FRIENDSHIP CIRCLES

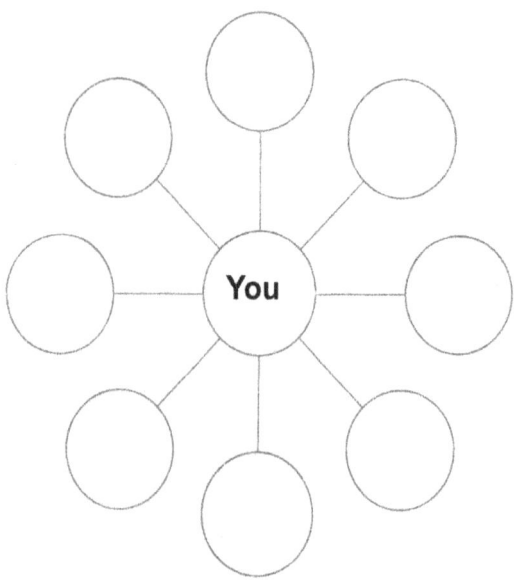

1. In the center circle, place your name.
2. In the circles that surround the circle where your name is placed, write the names of people that you know who are nonchurched, people who are your friends, neighbors, coworkers, people who you attend school with, associates, and relatives.
3. Select the prospect that will most likely go to church with you.
4. List the strategy that you will use to bring the person you selected to Christ this year.

Returning Visitors

There are reasons why visitors don't return after the first visit to the church. A visitor may not be impressed by the pastor, they may not be moved spiritually by the choir, or they may experience unfriendliness of the members. If visitors aren't impressed by the pastor when visiting, rarely will they join the church. Considering all things being equal, three out of ten visitors (3:10 ratio) should join the church. When visitors return on a consistent basis, it indicates that they are likely considering uniting with the church.

It has been said that we are living in a post-denominational age. Even the statistics before us bear this out, although we seem to be in denial of this fact. As we become aware of the state of our church, we are reminded of the legend of the Phoenix bird that burned itself to death and rose again, fresh and young, from its ashes. Yes, we have that hope that God's church today can rise from its ashes. This will be the church of Christ, freed from arrogance, hypocrisy, greed, and institutionalism. This will be the real church that God intended it to be.

EXERCISE

There are four discipleship programs which have proven, through experience, to be effective in making disciples.

Match the correct discipleship program with the correct author by placing the correct number on the line next to the author of that discipleship program.

____ Evangelism Explosion   1. Rick Warren
____ Four Covenating Classes   2. Jack Hayward
____ Master Plan For   3. Charles & Win Arn
        Making Disciples
____ Cleansing Stream   4. Gerald Kennedy

EXERCISE

Pastors and members understand that traditional churches are resistant to change. There are several reasons why this is so.

List five reasons why members of traditional churches resist change.

1. _____

2. _____

3. _____

4. _____

5. _____

Chapter 3

THE CALL TO PREACH

A catastrophic event happened which caused a drastic change in the direction of my life. One evening after closing my business, I went home and retired to bed. About two A.M. the telephone rang and the caller identified herself as the telephone operator. She immediately asked if I owned Continental Boat Company. She then informed me that there were seven fire companies at my place of business. I quickly dressed and went directly to my place of business and observed that it was completely engulfed in flames. The fire companies were still frantically fighting the fire. Realizing there was nothing I could do, I returned to my residence. For the next ten hours, I sat on a couch in my home in a state of shock.

Later that evening, I returned to the location to survey the loss. In reality, there wasn't much to survey. As I became more focused, I began to consider two options that possibly would ease the pain and disappointment of my loss. Number one, I could call upon some old friends to give me some comfort, such as Old Taylor, and Old Grand-Dad. This was just a fleeting thought.

Within the city limits of Pasadena, there is a canyon with a stately structure spanning it. This bridge has been unofficially dubbed "Suicide Bridge." This site is where many have solved their problems during the past years. This was also just a fleeting thought.

Then there came to mind a second option. *Return to church.* I remembered the brother who came by my shop regularly and chatted with me and would encourage me to come back to church. With time on my hands, I decided to return to church, the church where I had spent my young adult years. So, after some 14 years I returned to Calvary CME Church in Pasadena, California. I was surprised and humbled by the warm reception which I received from the members.

Pastor Hashaway immediately asked me to coach the church basketball team. At the University of Arkansas, I was a member of the track team. I informed the pastor that basketball was not my sport. Pastor Hashaway laughed and responded, "Don't worry, they just need an adult to be in charge. They will coach themselves." He was 100 percent correct because these boys won the Church League Championship their first year.

Through some unknown source, the pastor learned that many of the boys on the team were not members of the church. Pastor called me in for a conference regarding this situation. I was somewhat nervous, so I began to prepare my defense because I hadn't asked permission to use nonmembers on the team. Finally, I decided to go in and just ask for forgiveness.

I was quite relieved as this approach worked very well. I've learned that sometimes it is more expedient to venture without asking permission because the option of asking for forgiveness is always there. Pastor Hashaway informed me that the boys would have to attend church in order to participate in this athletic program. I relayed this information to the team, but at the same time, I presented an alternative. The alternative was if I would teach a Sunday class, would they agree to come to Sunday School? They agreed without any hesitation. This alternative was presented to the pastor who also agreed. One can probably imagine how noisy this Sunday School class of approximately 30 teenagers was.

The girls who also came to the class organized a cheerleaders group. Because of this class, the other Sunday School teachers seemed to assume a certain attitude when in my presence. Could this be because this class of teens was the noisiest in the Sunday School? They never made any verbal comments about the noise in my presence (I'm not so sure of comments they may have made in my absence, however). The kids were having a great deal of fun in the class and looked forward to this weekly experience. They really enjoyed coming to Sunday School as it was an exciting event. Nearing the end of this season, we learned that we had made the play-off. The whole church was overjoyed with the accomplishment of our team.

At the end of the season we were matched with a team from South Central Los Angeles to be in the play-off for the championship. The odds were heavily in favor of this team since it had won several league championships in the past. At this point, we were just happy to be in the play-off. Even though we had made the play-off, we were not completely convinced that we could defeat this team.

The week before the play-off was spent in practice and planning our strategy. Wisdom dictated that the play-off would be played on neutral turf. Marshal High School, located in the northwest area of Los Angeles, was designated as the play-off site.

The day of the play-off finally arrived. The excitement was at a high pitch. The pom-pom teams from both churches were there in their uniforms. Pastors and members of the various district churches were there to support the youth. Our team won the championship in overtime.

One Sunday afternoon, a social event took place in the Fellowship Hall. Rev. T. P. Lee, a visiting pastor, approached me and initiated a conversation concerning the church. He eventually made a statement which seemed unrelated to the ensuing conservation. He stated, "Brother Tollette, I've been observing you for some time and I am sure that you are being called to preach. In fact, you will accept this call very soon." His statement took me by complete surprise. After giving serious thought to this statement, I wondered if this was a confirmation of my call to the ministry.

I decided to go into a period of fasting and prayer. It seems that I could always pray more fervently in crisis situations. To me, this was the beginning of a turning point in my life. After spending a considerable time in serious prayer, I was convinced that my call was really from God. Several sessions of counseling were arranged with my pastor, Rev. Hashaway, regarding this important decision. Early in the first session, I informed him that I believed God was calling me to be a preacher. I told him how for several years I had been resisting this call. Pastor Hashaway gave me some wise counsel concerning entering the ministry.

Sanford B. Tollette, my older brother, had pastored several churches in the South Arkansas Conference and always had been my mentor and was also a great inspiration in my life. He was always available when there were critical decisions to be made in my life. It was natural that I would discuss this matter with him. I made flight arrangements to go to Little Rock, Arkansas, to discuss this situation with him. He seemed rather pleased that I had made this decision, even though I had mixed feelings about it. He continued to give wise counsel concerning the pastoral ministry. Not only did he encourage me, he also talked about some of the challenges and disappointments I would experience as a pastor. At this time, I had no desire to be a pastor; my objective was to function as a staff minister.

My pastor continued to assign me to different ministry tasks to give me an overall understanding of the different areas of ministry. As time passed, I served as a steward, director of Christian education, and lay leader. I was gaining invaluable experience in different areas of church organization.

This appointment proved to be significant in my ministerial development. Christian education was the area of involvement in my professional area of expertise. I proceeded to develop a tutorial program, which was a joint venture with one of the schools of the Pasadena Unified School District. Several teachers from one of the high schools committed several hours a week to our tutorial program. Each Wednesday afternoon, one of the Little League football teams would forgo their football practice and come to our church to be tutored in reading and math. This program serviced students from elementary through high school. Brother Thurman Holliday, a member of Calvary, and also a reading coordinator for the Los Angeles City School System, was instrumental in structuring our reading program.

During this period, I was also serving as a math coordinator for the Los Angeles City Schools. It was my responsibility to structure the math program. We averaged about 75 students daily in this weekly program. In the meantime, we planned to extend this program to include ten churches. We were funded $60,000 for the purpose of running a pilot program before proceeding to plan for expansion during the summer months.

Every experience we encounter in life has either positive or negative aspects. The question which should be asked is what was learned from each of these experiences. First, we learned that compromise is sometime expedient for the good of all concerned. As a leader, a pastor will be confronted with many difficult situations which will require compromising. When the youth were given an alternative regarding church membership, they bought into this alternative, which was to attend Sunday School, which was an excellent learning situation. Second, the lesson learned was we can use other things which youth are interested in to teach positive values for living. Athletics served as a bridge in making them active in a learning situation.

The annual California conference convenes during the second week of August. I was elected as a delegate to represent the church. Pastor Hashaway was called upon to give his report in the first business section. I was surprised he mentioned the tutorial program that we were engaged in. His report was well-received, and many questions were asked how we organized this program. Many of the questions focused on how they could replicate the program in their churches.

On the third day of the conference, the presiding elder approached me and informed me that the bishop desired to have a conference with me on Thursday. He also informed me that the bishop had decided that he would assign me to a church as pastor. Before I could respond to his statement, the elder instructed me to say "yes." Being assigned as pastor hadn't even crossed my mind.

Sure enough, on Thursday, I was summoned to a conference with the bishop. The presiding prelate was Bishop Norris S. Curry, a very learned man and one of the greatest preachers in the Methodist tradition. I had known him as the pastor of Phillips Temple, our first church in Los Angeles. A district lay training session was being held at his church, and I was one of the presenters. After my presentation, Dr. Curry made a critique of my effort which at that time did not seem to be positive. Later, as I learned more about this pastor, I developed an attitude of admiration and respect for this great theologian.

Upon entering his office, we exchanged the usual formal greeting. Bishop Curry came directly to the issue at hand. He said, "Brother Tollette, I've been observing you for some time, and I am impressed with your ministry. I have decided to appoint you as pastor of Emmanuel Temple Church, in Victorville, California. What do you think of this idea?"

I answered, "Bishop, I am appreciative of the confidence that you have in me, and I assure you that I will do my very best be a good pastor."

Traditionally, the last day of the conference is when the pastoral appointments are read. As usual, the church was completely filled. This event was something that I had witnessed all my life, but something different was about to happen. I was anxiously waiting to hear my name called as a pastor. I think I will always remember these words spoken by Bishop Norris S. Curry: "Emmanuel Temple, Victorville, Rev. C. B. Tollette, Pastor." At this point, I felt that I had come full circle in my ministry. All of my past experiences such as classroom teacher, mental health counselor, master training teacher, 14 years of operating my own business, and four years training as a community organizer by the Industrial Areas Foundation were about to be used in my pastorate.

Chapter 4

ENTERING THE ITINERATE MINISTRY

The annual conference convened in Oakland, California, and at the closing, I received my Certificate of Appointment. With this official document in hand, I was anxious to return to Southern California to be briefed by the officers of my charge. Sometime later, I became aware that they had already received the news that I was assigned as their pastor. About two or three hours after the appointments were read, I learned that they had put together a complete unofficial dossier of my activities and qualifications.

Victorville was a 100-mile drive from my home in Pasadena, California. I decided to make this trip to Victorville Saturday morning for a briefing of the state of the church. Again, I found myself driving through the Cajon Pass to enter the high desert where the small town of Victorville was located in this barren area which was the habitat of rattlesnakes and Joshua trees. It was apparent that the Joshua trees were the original inhabitants of this area. The population of this town was 14,000. The Joshua trees and rattlesnakes had homesteaded and made this place their domain long before it was populated by people. Apparently, there were not enough residents to challenge their claim.

The homely appearance of the Joshua tree indicated that this specimen really needed protection. Therefore, the United States Forest Service protected it by declaring it an endangered species. The rattlesnake had no need of this protection as it had mutated into a deadly viper and was now known as the Mojave Green. Through the process of mutation, it was able to adapt to the extreme temperatures of the high desert. It has the reputation of being one of the most poisonous snakes in California.

The three officers who met to brief me on the state of the church informed me that the church had just recently moved to this location. The directions given took me to the outer edge of the northern boundary of the town.

When the church came within view, I was pleasantly surprised because it appeared to be recently built. I was familiar with the old structure because I had visited Victorville with Pastor Lee about two years before. It was somewhat unusual for a pastor's first appointment to be a new, attractive building with a seating capacity of approximately 250 with plenty of parking. Not only was I surprised, I was also impressed with this new building.

Three church officers were waiting for me as I arrived at about 11 A.M. We proceeded to the small church office where the briefing would take place. One of the officers opened the meeting with this statement: "Pastor, we have some good news and some bad news. Which do you want first?"

My preference was to hear the bad news first as I thought the good news would raise my spirits after hearing the bad news. The next statement from the chairman of the Steward Board was, "The bad news is we don't have a penny in the treasury. The good news is we don't owe anybody anything." Not having any money didn't pose any great problem to me because of my enthusiasm of being assigned to my first charge. Perhaps my naivety and lack of experience accounted for this unrealistic optimism.

After the officers completed a thorough assessment of the congregation, we proceeded outside to survey the five acres of church property. I was also impressed with the foresight of this congregation in purchasing this amount of property. The congregation was assured that there would be adequate space for parking as the membership increases. The sanctuary was simple, but it was clean and attractive.

Principle #3: Churches grow when there is an attractive, clean facility, with satisfactory parking space and adequate seating capacity

We concluded the briefing within two hours, and I began the two-hour drive back to my home. The chore before me was to prepare my first sermon as I wanted to make a positive impression on the congregation.

On my journey back home, I thought about Rev. T. P. Lee, who founded this church 23 years previously. This pastor and his wife had driven from Los Angeles on a two-lane highway through the Cajon Pass every week to pastor this congregation. This was certainly a display of a rare commitment to ministry and a love for the members of the church and the people of the community of Victorville.

Principle #4: The leadership strength of the pastor and favorable transition of pastors is a prime factor in growing a church

I arrived at the church at about 9 A.M. Sunday. I didn't take part in any of the proceedings because I thought it might be wise for me to observe how they operated on Sunday mornings. There were about 12 adults and about five children in Sunday School. The attendance for the worship service was 30 persons, even though the reported membership was 129.

For the next six years, I formed the habit of recording the attendance and offerings of every gathering of the church. The choir and ushers were in place to start the 11 A.M. service. I was very pleased to see this happen. We proceeded through the preliminary activities of the worship service. After the announcements were made, I decided that this would be an appropriate time to make my general comments. As I rose to make my comments, my first statement was, "You have a new pastor." I thought for a moment and then added, "I have never pastored before." At this point, Mrs. Ivese Thomas, an 82-year-old senior who was regarded as the matriarch of this congregation, rose from her seat and made this statement. "Son, we will all grow together." This statement by the matriarch of the congregation was an affirmation of my pastorate. After this statement by Mrs. Thomas, the members seemed very positive in accepting me as pastor. It was no accident that this lady rose to make this statement. I feel that it was the providence of God.

This was the beginning of six-year tenure as pastor. In reality, I was under no illusion that having a Certificate of Appointment in hand made me their pastor. I realized that it would take considerable time to establish myself as pastor in their hearts. I hadn't earned the position as yet. This was an exciting growing experience for both me and the congregation.

It was only natural with my background in public education that teaching would become a major emphasis in my ministry. In my own estimation, preaching would not be my strongest point in pastoring. One interesting point to be made about my preaching happened at the close of one of our worship services. There was always an usher stationed beside the pulpit as I was preaching. I wasn't quite sure why she was stationed in this position. Later at the close of the worship service, she approached me and said, "Pastor, I don't think you understand why I stand next to the pulpit during the worship service. Well, I am the pastor's usher, and I'm supposed to bring your coat after you finish preaching, but you haven't preached upon a sweat yet." I assured her that I would take care of this situation.

As time passed, I was able to learn more about the history of this church and how they had overcome almost impossible situations. Through all of these difficulties, the members maintained their faith that their church would survive.

Ms. Thomas was one of the members who attended the annual conference each year consistently. For several years, she would stand outside of the bishop's office, hoping to get an audience on behalf of the Victorville congregation. On one occasion, as she was standing in her usual position outside of the bishop's office hoping to speak with the bishop, she overheard the presiding elder talking with another pastor. The presiding elder made this statement. "This lady has been coming to the annual conference every year asking for help to build a church in Victorville. We're not even thinking about investing any money in that little town in the middle of the desert." Mrs. Thomas responded in a rather abrupt tone. "This church will be there when you are dead and gone." She then noticed that the bishop was leaving his office, and she quickly introduced herself and stated that she had been trying to get an appointment with him for several years.

The bishop invited her into his office where she could present her concerns. Obviously, the bishop was more impressed by her faith and commitment than he was with the idea of investing in a small church in the desert. After listening to her story, the bishop presented the church with a challenge which he probably thought would be impossible for them to achieve in that particular time span. "If your congregation will raise $20,000 within three months, I will match that amount." Mrs. Thomas was elated with this commitment by the bishop. She neglected to inform him, however, that the church had the $20,000 in the building fund treasury at this particular time.

Even today, I am not sure whether this was an oversight or if it was a temporary intentional lapse of memory. I'm reminded of a story in the Gospel of Matthew when a Canaanite woman approached Jesus and asked him to cast a devil out of her daughter. This lady was quite persistent in her appeal to Jesus. Eventually Jesus granted her request. Jesus answered and said unto her, "O, woman, great is thy faith; be it unto thee even as thou wilt. And her daughter was made whole from that very hour" (Matthew 15:28).

Within the time span of three months, Pastor T. P. Lee and a representative number of officers from Emmanuel Temple Church traveled to Los Angeles and presented the bishop with a certified check for $20,000. It would be difficult to describe the bishop's surprise, for he had believed that this was an impossible task of this church. "With men, this is impossible; but with God all things are possible" (Matthew 19:26).

Bishop Walter H. Amos, the presiding bishop of the Ninth Episcopal District, called a meeting of the pastors and laypersons of the conference. He proceeded to make a passionate presentation of the opportunity to develop the church in Victorville, California. After discussing the project and answering all pertinent questions, the bishop was able to raise the $20,000 as he had promised. This was the beginning of the fulfillment of Pastor Lee's dream which began 23 years previously. This pastor had actually traveled a two-lane highway through rain, sleet, and snow for 23 years to pastor this small congregation in the high desert. This was certainly an unusual display of faith and commitment. He had become highly respected and loved by almost everyone in the community. This was the pastor who had predicted some three years before that I would become a pastor.

Emmanuel Temple was located approximately 2 miles from George Air Force Base. On many occasions, I was invited to preach on the base chapel. The congregation enjoyed the fellowship with the Gospel Service at the base. Many of the military personnel began to worship with our church. Sgt. Moore and his wife, Gail, eventually joined Emmanuel Temple. He was licensed to preach by the Church of God in Christ. This was a real blessing in that

Rev. Moore had several special ministry gifts such as preaching, leadership, and administration. This turned out to be a most important addition to our ministry staff. Adding staff is one of the church principles which ensures growth.

Principle #5: Organizing small groups and delegating leadership enhances church growth

During the second year of my tenure, I realized that we needed more children and youth in our Sunday School. I observed several buses picking up children for Sunday School in our community. The idea of buying a bus seemed to be the right way to increase our Sunday School. A considerable amount of time was devoted to researching how to organize a bus ministry. The result of this study indicated that a bus was more suitable than a van to develop a bus ministry. Churches usually purchase vans and use them more as a shuttle service in bringing people to church and returning them to their homes after worship.

With a great amount of enthusiasm, I requested the Official Board to buy a bus. Up until this point, the church had not refused anything that I had asked. To my surprise, the board voted against my request to buy a bus. This denial was the first in my administration. It was quite disappointing, but it was probably a good thing that happened.

During the next week, Ms. Jones, who was an administrator for the phone company, requested a conference to discuss an issue with me. She asked how I felt about the Official Board denying my request to purchase a bus in my last official meeting. I admitted that I was really disappointed in being denied my request because I had invested a considerable amount of time in researching the feasibility of such a ministry. She replied, "Pastor, may I make a suggestion regarding this situation?" My answer was yes. Ms. Jones suggested that I write up a proposal detailing how the bus would be used and how this would make a positive impact on the ministry of the church. Immediately, a light went on in my mind as I realized this was the piece that was missing in my previous presentation.

At the closing of the Wednesday Bible Study, I asked Rev. Moore if he would remain because I had something important to discuss with him. I related my desire to initiate a bus ministry, but I needed a detailed proposal explaining how the bus would be used to bring new members into the church. As I related this to him, I noticed that a smile appeared on his face. He then informed me that he and Gail, his wife, were working on such a proposal at this particular time.

The next week after the Wednesday evening Bible Study, he and Gail placed in my hand a completed proposal for a bus ministry. It was very well written. We engaged in a discussion concerning how to present the purposes and goals of a bus ministry. Two weeks later, I presented this proposal to the church conference. It was accepted unanimously.

Every challenge we face in life, whether it be pleasant or unpleasant, has within it a lesson to be learned. What was learned in this situation? The first thing is sometimes what we feel is a defeat, in reality, is a valuable lesson learned. The second lesson learned is that an issue must be presented in such a way that all anticipated questions are answered in the presentation. These lessons have remained with me throughout my ministry.

The next Sunday, three officers of the church came to my office and asked if I could be available after the worship service. I informed them that I would be available. The officers added that this would include dinner, as they were aware that my wife and I would have to drive back to Pasadena. After service, a three-car convoy was formed and the first stop was at a service station in an adjacent suburb of Hesperia. We parked the automobiles and walked over where a bus was parked with a for sale sign on it. The owner asked if we would like to take it for a test run. Since Rev. Moore had a military license to drive buses and trucks, we decided to take it on a test run.

After taking it for a trial spin, the officers asked if I liked this vehicle. The officers probably were aware of my enthusiasm and before I could answer, they suggested that there were two other vehicles to check. We then proceeded to the next stop to inspect the next vehicle. We didn't take this bus for a test drive, but we did start the engine. The officers did not show any degree of interest in this particular vehicle; therefore, we proceeded to the final location where we would observe the third vehicle.

This vehicle appeared to be in a much better condition than the other two we had observed. We decided to take this one on a test run. It was relatively quiet, and the interior appeared as if it had been refurbished. I really liked this vehicle better than the previous two that we had tested. The officers then asked which of the three vehicles I would prefer. At this point I was so delighted that they had decided to buy a bus that I chose the cheapest one. The chairman of the trustee board answered, "Pastor, you don't want either of the previous two that we looked at; *this* is the one that you want." Again, I was surprised, because this was the most expensive one of the three. It was obvious that the case was closed as I offered no rebuttal to the officer's decision.

The next Sunday as I came in view of our church, I observed a newly painted vehicle with the name Emmanuel Temple Church displayed on both sides of the bus. It was now up to me to fulfill the promises that I had made about bringing new members into the church. The more important point was that a new ministry was being organized.

Each Saturday, Rev. Moore and his wife, Gail, would canvass the community by making personal contacts with families. Rev Moore's main responsibility was driving the bus, and Gail served as the coordinator of this ministry. An impressive database was being developed that included the names of the parents, number of children in the family, their names, ages, and phone numbers. Parents were required to sign a permission form before the children could ride the bus. Also, the parents would receive a document explaining the rules of conduct for children and the times of pickup and return. Each week, the number of children participating in this ministry grew in numbers. Finally, it was necessary to conduct a Sunday School class on the bus as we didn't have enough room in the church to accommodate the numbers of children coming to Sunday School.

Principle #6: Growth occurs when marketing techniques are utilized

One result of this ministry was a number of parents united with the church. The bus ministry functioned for two-and-a-half years.

One evening before Bible Study, Rev. Moore placed a document for a prison ministry on my desk. He explained that he had had met with the installation chaplain of the California Institution for Men, usually referred to as Chino State Prison. In this meeting, he had received the necessary information regarding how to start a prison ministry. He was even offered a choice of days when he would like to participate in this ministry. The prison chaplain reviewed the rules and regulations that groups would have to understand and abide by when they come to minister to the "residents" of this facility. Rev. Moore had received commitments of approximately 30 persons, mostly young adults, from the Victorville community to participate in this ministry. These individuals were from the various churches of the city.

The last point to be covered was for me, as senior pastor, to visit the facility and meet with the installation chaplain. During this briefing session, the chaplain reviewed the rules and regulations for persons and groups coming in to do ministry. The chaplain spent a considerable time in this briefing relating how impressed he was with my associate minister, Rev. Moore.

After all details of the preliminary planning were completed, those who had signed up for this ministry were required to attend a meeting at Emmanuel Temple to be briefed on the procedures and regulations regarding groups who wish to minister in this facility. All 30 people who had committed to this ministry were present at this meeting. I made brief opening comments, then turned the meeting over to Rev. Moore, who initiated this ministry.

The church bus was made available as transportation for this ministry as the facility was about 40 miles from Victorville. The ministry would meet at Emmanuel Temple on the second Tuesday of each week for prayer before traveling to the Chino facility. This ministry was in operation for approximately two years.

Eventually, Rev. Moore received orders to be assigned to the Far East Command (this was really being assigned to Korea). Emmanuel Temple was saddened in losing this committed young preacher. After Rev. Moore arrived in Korea, he organized a worship service and named it the Emmanuel Mission Outreach Service. He sent offerings regularly to Emmanuel Temple. He also documented the activities that this mission service performed and mailed this information to Emmanuel Temple on a regular basis.

Within a week, I received an urgent call from the installation chaplain regarding Rev. Moore's orders. He asked if I would be willing to come to the prison for a conference with him as there was an important issue that he would like to discuss with me. I agreed to do so.

I arrived at the facility the next afternoon for this meeting. Chaplain Stevens came right to the point of this meeting. He stated that Rev. Moore had informed him that he would be transferred to Korea within a month. He also stated that this ministry was one of the most effective ministries in the facility and he would be disappointed to lose it.

At this point, I was not aware of what the chaplain was leading up to. Therefore, I asked, "Chaplain, what does this have to do with me?"

He replied, "As I indicated earlier, I don't want to lose this ministry; therefore, I will make you a proposition. I am prepared to offer you a 20-hour per week position as a state prison chaplain. This ministry would be your primary responsibility to manage. Pastor, I have been praying that you would agree to this proposal."

Considering the time that Rev. Moore and the group had invested in this ministry, and also the chaplain's plea, I accepted this proposition immediately. We proceeded to do the necessary paperwork immediately. I needed to have the results of a physical examination from my health carrier sent over. I was now a prison chaplain for the State of California. This turned out to be a most rewarding experience and a valuable entry in my repertoire. My assigned duties included teaching, counseling, scheduling services, and even performing marriages.

Principle #7: Churches grow as they participate in the social arena and make good relationships with city officials and local residents

The Bell Mountain Incident

Pastoral visits included a community further north of the city. This community derived its name from a steep elevation of land rising approximately 1,000 feet above the desert floor. The natural shape of this formation resembled a bell, thus, the name "Bell Mountain." Apparently most of the residents of this community chose to live in this area as most of them owned horses. This community was approximately four or five miles from the center of the city.

The families had children and realized that some type of recreational facility was needed. The residents of the community met and decided to build a recreational facility for their youth. Then, over a period, a youth facility was built. The residents of the community raised the finances for the land and construction of a recreation facility. This facility served as a meeting place where teens could "hang out" and enjoy fellowship with each other. Of course, parents always supervised them.

As the youth finished high school, many left because of limited work opportunities in Bell Mountain. Many moved on to Las Vegas, or south to Los Angeles for work or to continue their education. So, over a period of time, there were no youth left to use this facility. It remained vacant for a number of years. Finally, Mrs. Ivese Thomas, a longtime resident of the community, contacted the San Bernardino County offices and offered to turn this property over to the county with one stipulation. This stipulation stated that if the property was ever listed on the market for sale, Emmanuel Temple Church would have the first option to purchase it. This proved to be a strategic move on the part of the residents of Bell Mountain.

During the second year of my pastorate, the church was in an exciting stage of growth. Several ministries were added, and many people in the community were uniting with the church. One Wednesday evening as I traveled to Victorville to teach Bible Study, there was a letter from the San Bernardino County office on my desk. As I opened the letter, I assumed that it was a tax statement of some type. The letter stated that the property in Bell Mountain was now up for sale. The letter also stated that

Emmanuel Temple has the right to exercise their option of buying it first. I suspected they didn't expect this small congregation would be able to buy this property.

The following Sunday, I called the trustees and stewards to meet with me after church. The letter was read at this meeting, and a lively discussion ensued. The officers were not comfortable with the idea of buying this property. They really couldn't see that it had any value. As pastor, I could not see any real value in this property either, but I did suspect that there was some reason for it being up for sale at this time. The trustees suggested that we respond before the 20-day period expired. We also asked that the county provide us with more details concerning this property. Considering the fact that this parcel of land had not been used for any purpose for several years, there had to be some reason the property was now up for sale.

The asking price of $20,000 for these five acres of land seemed very reasonable. The more I thought about the situation, the more my thoughts focused on buying the Bell Mountain property. In the meantime, I called another general meeting of the officers and other leaders of the church. The purpose of this meeting was to present a proposal in detail of the pros and cons of buying this property. The group posed a series of relevant questions which were answered. I suggested that if 20 people would agree to advance $1,000, we could buy this property. As the pastor, I was the first to write a check for $1,000. Nineteen more people immediately followed this lead, and within half an hour, we raised $20,000.

The next week, I travel to the San Bernardino County office and presented them with a cashier's check for $20,000. There's no way to describe the surprise on their faces when I informed them that I was presenting the check for the purchase of the Bell Mountain property. It was such a surprise that they seemed confused about what they should do next. They passed my check around and thoroughly examined it.

Eventually, the question was asked if the church really wanted to buy this property (I thought it was obvious that this was our intent). We were given the required forms to be completed so that the deed could be transferred to Emmanuel Temple. We soon received the deed to the property by mail. Emmanuel Temple was now the owner of another five acres of land. The members were still somewhat apprehensive about the whole situation. They were probably fearful that the church would find it difficult to rid itself of this land which they considered useless. They also wondered if the church would be responsible for repaying the $20,000 to the members who had loaned the money to the church.

Knowing and understanding their reticence, I announced publicly that I would personally buy this parcel of land if it was not sold within a year. This statement seemed to have relieved most of their fears of being saddled with five acres of land with no value.

Next, it was necessary to form an ad hoc committee that would administrate and manage this property until it was sold. They seemed relieved after this announcement was made. There was one other issue that was prominent in my mind. Many in the congregation didn't understand why we would purchase this property even though we felt that we had covered all of their concerns. Within a very short time, this question was answered. The airport in Apple Valley needed this land for a landing approach for future planning to accommodate increased air traffic. This would serve as an approach lane for planes landing at the airport. This was the real reason why the land was to be put on the market to be sold. This shed new light on the whole process, as this provided the church an advantage in negotiating when we would sell it.

In exactly three weeks, we received our first bid on this property for $30,000. Being privy to the information concerning the airport, we immediately rejected this bid. Several of the officers were in favor of accepting this first bid, although the majority agreed not to accept. The officers were now confident that the investment was more secure. During the next nine weeks, three other bids were presented for $40,000, $50,000, and $60,000. We accepted the last bid of $60,000 as I was unable to convince the officers to hold out any longer.

The ad hoc committee continued to work out the details of this sale. Emmanuel Temple eventually received a check in the amount of $60,000 for full payment of the property. A special meeting of the steward board, trustee board, and ad hoc committee was called to repay those who had advanced the $20,000. Before the treasurer issued the checks, she made a statement that was most appropriate. She said, "We have learned something important. If we follow leadership and cooperate with each other, there is nothing that we cannot accomplish." She then proceeded to pass out the checks. We had dinner together that night and enjoyed and celebrated our accomplishment. The church conference voted that the proceeds of this sale would be used to liquidate the mortgage on the church.

Principle #4: The leadership strength of the pastor and favorable transition of pastors is a prime factor in growing a church

EXERCISE

How can a person be sure that he/she is being called to preach? Circle A, B, C, D, or E as your answer.

A. Read relevant passages of the Bible.
B. Seek counsel from a preacher or someone you feel is capable of giving wise counsel.
C. Set a specific time devoted to fasting and prayer asking God's guidance.
D. If married, discuss the issue with your mate.
E. All of the above.

Chapter 5

MINISTRY AT RIVERSIDE

At the closing of the conference in 1982, I was assigned as pastor of Amos Temple Church in Riverside, California. A short time before the conference convened, I met with Bishop Cummins and requested that I be assigned to a church closer to home. The bishop informed me that I would be assigned as pastor of Riverside, California. My immediately response was that this was not a very good assignment for me. After a very brief discussion of this issue, the bishop said emphatically, "Brother Tollette, you are going to Riverside or nowhere." For six years I had pastored a church 100 miles from where I resided and this had taken quite a toll on my health and certainly my automobiles.

The congregation had ambivalent feelings concerning this assignment as my style of preaching was quite different from the pastor I was following. The other reason was that Riverside was approximately 60 miles from my home. It was obvious that this assignment would also entail a considerable amount of traveling. In spite of ambivalent feelings concerning this assignment, I arrived at the church at about nine o'clock Sunday morning. A brief time was spent talking with several of the officers who were anxiously awaiting my arrival.

I suggested that they carry on as usual, as I did not want to interfere with their procedures at this point. One of the officers took me on a quick tour of the facility to familiarize me with how the church was laid out. I was also able to observe the classes which were in session. This provided a convenient opportunity to make a cursory evaluation of the condition of the facility. This brief tour of the facility was not a positive experience as the church was in need of major repairs. The sanctuary was small with a seating capacity of about one hundred persons. The restrooms were in the basement adjacent to the kitchen, the pews in the sanctuary were not very stable, and the walls were stained, which indicated that the roof was leaking. Wisdom dictated that this would not be an appropriate time to make mention of these things.

There was one positive thing, however. They had a fantastic gospel choir. I asked that the church come back Monday evening so we could begin to plan and make an assessment of the things to be taken care of immediately. After the worship service, I was invited to the home of one of the members to enjoy a seven-course dinner. Truly, this was an awesome experience.

There was one condition that had to be addressed immediately, and that was the location of the pastor's office. Currently, the pastor's study was in the basement, and this location did not provide a conducive atmosphere for counseling and other pastoral duties. At the mention of this, a quietness came over the audience and a nondescript expression appeared on the faces of the members of the conference. I concluded that it would not be wise to pursue this issue at this particular time either.

After returning on the following Wednesday for Bible Study, the pastor's office had been moved upstairs to a more conducive location. I was very pleased that this had happened. Certain other upgrades and improvements were made such as a new ceiling, new light fixtures, and new carpeting. I was also impressed with how much they accomplished in a very short time. It was obvious that this venture had been well planned and coordinated.

The next several weeks were devoted to improving the infrastructure of the church. An evaluation of the existing ministries was done, and certain changes and modifications were put into effect. One of the first items of restructuring was the establishment of a Leadership Academy. Chairman of boards, auxiliaries, and small groups were required to attend this four-week seminar. I was pleasantly surprised that at least 90 percent attendance was achieved. The positive effects of this seminar played an important part in establishing teaching as a priority in making disciples. This approach to ministry assures both numerical and spiritual growth of the congregation. Yes, numbers do count because numbers represent people.

The Wednesday night Bible Study continued to grow, as it began to attract not only the members of the church but also members of the community. The attendance averaged between 30 and 40 persons each session. This was an impressive accomplishment for a church of 200 members.

Several members approached me and suggested that they would be interested in attending a noon Bible Study. I was receptive to this idea as it provided an opportunity to reach more people by creating a new small group. The next Sunday, I announced that a noon Bible Study would begin on Wednesday of this week. Twelve people were in attendance for this first meeting. Mrs. Bertram, a member of the community, attended this first meeting. She became a regular attendee. She also displayed an unusual knowledge and understanding of the Bible. Her participation in the discussions and her knowledge of the scriptures enhanced the learning of the students. It was obvious that Ms. Bertrand possessed the gift of knowledge and teaching. The Bible teaches that all Christians have at least one spiritual gift. "… When he ascended on high, he led captives in his train and gave gifts to men" (Ephesians 4:8).

There were periods when Mrs. Bertram would be absent from the Bible Study. But she would always reappear after these brief absences.

A conference was arranged with Ms. Bertrand to learn more about her background and other involvements. Her training came through a mainline denomination although she wasn't attached to any particular church at this time. It became clear why she attended the Amos Temple worship service on a regular basis. She organized an Outreach Missionary ministry to Haiti. Mrs. Bertram was very creative in how she developed this ministry and was able to enlist the participation of other partners.

Each three-month period, Ms. Bertrand would collect clothes and canned goods from various churches. She contacted different types of stores who contributed various items to pack these materials for shipping. One of the major airlines would ship these packages of food and clothing every three months to Haiti at no cost. I recognized an unusual opportunity to add a new ministry to the church. I suggested to Ms. Bertram that we would welcome her to base this ministry at Amos Temple. She was elated with this suggestion as she now had a place where she could house her ministry on a permanent basis. A new small group was formed to assist in administering this ministry. It was appropriately called the "Haitian Airlift."

It was quite demanding for me, as pastor, to travel the 120-mile round-trip to Riverside each Wednesday for the midday Bible Study. Therefore, I asked Ms. Bertram if she would she be interested in teaching the Wednesday noon Bible Study. She agreed to do this without any hesitation. Ms. Bertram became a valuable addition to the teaching staff at the church. Approximately 50 people attended the various the Bible Studies every week. Twenty percent of the membership was engaged in weekly Bible Study.

Principle #7: Churches grow as they participate in the social arena and make good relationships with city officials and local residents

Amos Temple had now entered an impressive growing mode; in fact, the sanctuary was now approximately 95 percent full. One of the principles of church growth states that when the sanctuary is 80 percent full, another service must be added. I discussed with some of the officers about my intention of starting a new service at 8 A.M. on Sundays. I was surprised at the negative reaction from these officers. Knowing that the growth would level off because of a lack of space in the sanctuary, I was determined to start an 8 A.M. service. At the next church conference, I presented a proposal explaining the advantages and disadvantages for creating a new service.

Even though the proposal was presented in such a way that all anticipated questions were answered, many of the members were just basically against another the second service. Most pastors are aware of the resistance that they face when a new worship service is introduced. There may be several reasons why members resist a second service: (1) the added cost of maintaining a second service (2) members like to see a full house in worship. Today, people are more mobile and have the option of doing other things on Sunday. Therefore, many people prefer to worship at an early-morning service, then have the rest of the day to do other things. Whether we admit it or not, we are in competition with other activities on Sunday.

In spite of initial resistance, the 8 A.M. service was initiated. At the end of the month, an average of 50 individuals were attending the eight o'clock service. It was somewhat surprising that the tithes and offering in the eight o'clock service was a much higher percentage than in the eleven o'clock service. It might be a good idea to do an analysis regarding the attendance at eight and eleven. The record of attendance and finances showed that there was consistent growth in both worship services.

As the church was in a positive growth mode, I saw a need to bring on a person to develop the youth and young adult ministries. I had suggested this idea to a number of the key officers and members of the church. Unfortunately, this idea wasn't received with any enthusiasm by the officers. Apparently more work needed to be done before this could be implemented.

Churches Grow as They Organize for Growth by Adding Staff

Amos Temple experienced unusual growth during this period. Pastor C. C. Coleman, a very good friend, and I usually enjoyed having breakfast together at least once each week. During one of the breakfast meetings, the conversation evolved around associate ministers. I mentioned that I didn't have any help in the pulpit and needed an associate minister. Pastor Coleman mentioned that he had about seven associate ministers and really didn't have room to seat them all in the pulpit. I recognized that this was an opportunity that I could not pass up. Pastor Coleman suggested that he would consider loaning one of his associates to Amos Temple for a period of one year. A few days later, I received a phone call from a Rev. Willy McDaniel saying that his pastor had suggested that he call to make an appointment.

We met the following week. At this meeting, Rev. McDaniel presented himself with humility and at the same time a sense of assurance. He had a broad knowledge of church organization and structure. At the end of the conference, I invited him to preach on the coming Sunday, which he accepted. The congregation was very impressed with the sermon that this young man preached.

In the next church conference, I proposed to the members that we should bring Rev. Mac on as a staff minister for three months on a trial basis. If he was not a benefit to the church during those three months, he would no longer be kept on the staff. Interestingly, during the trial period, the youth and young adults tripled in attendance.

When this trial period of three months ended, I suggested that since the trial period was over, it was time to close out this ministry as agreed upon. At this point, there was a loud verbal protest. People were ready to tar and feather me for suggesting that. They proceeded to vote unanimously to add him permanently to the staff. Rev. McDaniel was now officially the youth and young adult minister with a job description that defined his duties. Since we had two services, Rev. Mac would preach at least two times a month. Within three months, the youth and young adult department had grown threefold.

Principle #3: Churches grow when the facilities are attractive with clean restrooms

The rainy season in Southern California is usually in December through February and we were not prepared for this. As I arrived at the church one Sunday in a severe rainstorm, I was shocked to see the rain running down the walls of the sanctuary. This was just the beginning of an unusual Sunday as several crisis events took place during the worship service. As the choir was rendering their first inspirational number, a very loud bang was heard in the sanctuary, and even outside which sounded like a sonic boom. It didn't take long to locate from where this noise originated.

Right in the middle of the sanctuary a whole pew had given way and about 10 or 11 persons found themselves sitting on the floor. The service was interrupted for a few minutes as the men removed this broken pew from the sanctuary. We were now ready to continue our worship service. Next, there was some hesitation as the musician was having difficulty coaxing the organ to issue forth any sounds. Without any success, he walked over to the piano and discovered that something there was not working properly either. During this episode, I was struggling to maintain my composure as these chaotic events were taking place in a Sunday morning worship service. At the close of the service, I made a strong appeal for the congregation to meet Monday evening to deal with an important issue.

Upon arriving at the church on Monday evening, I observed that the sanctuary was filled with an impressive number of members. After a brief devotion, I asked the congregation to take just a few minutes to engage in silent prayer. Afterward, a summary of the three main areas of the facility to be addressed was presented, namely: 1. a new roof, 2. painting the interior, and 3. new pews. The highest priority was roofing. The trustees were directed to secure bids on the roof immediately.

Three bids were secured doing the week. As this was an emergency situation, the trustees signed the contract for the middle bid and the new roof was finished within seven days. The church conference empowered the office to pay $10,000 cash from the building fund.

The congregation was quite pleased when there were no leaks after the first rain. With this accomplishment, I decided that it was an opportune time to initiate plans to take care of the other pressing items while the enthusiasm and momentum was at a high pitch. I suggested that the church devise a plan to raise enough money to take care of the other items. The congregation endorsed this idea instantly. Ms. Brooks, a capable and committed member, stepped forward and volunteered to chair the building fund ministry. She was well respected and wielded an unusual amount of influence in the congregation. Within ten weeks, the building fund had grown to $60,000.

The church conference authorized the trustees to secure estimates to make certain improvements to the church. The estimates included the following: painting the interior of the church, purchasing new pews, purchasing new chairs for the choir, and relocating and redesigning the toilet facilities in the basement. It was discovered that this building was built on a landfill, and this presented a unique problem. There was an 18-inch drop from one end of the Fellowship Hall to the other end. This entailed completely dismantling everything in the basement and starting over from scratch. The whole project was completed in exactly eight weeks. It was obvious that the members took pride in their accomplishments during the year.

It is commonly accepted in church growth circles that three out of ten visitors should unite with the church. Visitors were returning on a consistent basis and at least one-third of the visitors united with the church. The church had not organized a particular marketing program although we determined through responsible documentation that members came to the church because friends or relatives had invited them. Research indicates that 85–90 percent of the visitors come to the church because they are invited by friends or relatives. It follows that any evangelistic outreach would not only teach the members how to share their faith, but also would encourage them to form relationships with those who are unchurched.

Principle #2: Churches grow when evangelism is the highest priority of the church

I have previously mentioned Marge, the proprietor of a beauty salon, who used it as an opportunity to invite or encourage people to attend her church. More than 30 individuals joined the church during the year because Marge had invited them. It was apparent that Marge was using her gift of evangelism in a unique type of witness. This type of outreach is sometimes referred to in church growth circles as "Relational Evangelism." It is much easier to share Jesus with others if a relationship is formed initially. Remember, members must be enthusiastic about the ministry of their church in order to effectively witness to others.

One morning when a friend and I were taking our daily walk, we met a young adult lady who engaged us in a conversation. This young lady was really on fire about the ministry of her church. She began to tell about all of the ministries of her church with a great amount of enthusiasm. In fact, my walking partner and I could hardly get a word in the conversation. In the end, she offered us an invitation to visit her church on the next Sunday. My friend and I identified with King Agrippa who replied when Paul was defending himself, "… Almost thou persuadest me to be a Christian" (Acts 26:28). Yes, we were almost persuaded to accept the invitation to visit her church. Through these types of encounters, we learn that there are many occasions which present opportunities to witness the Good News.

Principle #2: Churches grow through relational evangelism. Eighty-five percent of persons who unite with the church come by friends and relatives

At the end of the conference year, 91 people had united with Amos Temple and 27 baptisms had been performed. Also, two individuals accepted the call to preach and were issued licenses. This was a blessing since they could now qualify to participate in the worship service. It also offered an opportunity for them to gain experience in being assigned ministerial duties in the different departments of the church. During my five-year tenure at Amos Temple, 300 people had united with the church. With this moderate success, another opportunity presented itself.

I was offered a full-time position as Episcopal Director of Evangelism for the Ninth Episcopal District. Even though I had mixed feelings about leaving Riverside, I accepted the position. An excellent transition of pastors was made which assured continuity of growth and development of the church. In the ensuing years, this congregation grew to more than 1,100 members. Later, much more will be said about the pastor who succeeded me at Riverside.

After five years of driving 140 miles round-trip from Los Angeles to Riverside to pastor Amos Temple Church, I requested that I be assigned to a church nearer to my home. In the meantime, Bishop Nathaniel Lindsey was assigned to the Ninth

Episcopal District, who denied this request. This new bishop was committed to evangelism and church growth. Two alternatives were offered: (1) continue pastoring at Amos Temple, (2) accept the position of Episcopal Director of Evangelism. This would be a full-time position housed in the Episcopal office. I was elated with this second option as I was certified as a church growth consultant by the Fuller Evangelical Association. This training provided me the expertise to function in this position. I accepted this position without hesitation.

The Episcopal director's office was set up with furniture and other necessary items. The bishop and I devoted considerable time planning how this position would impact the churches in the Episcopal district. A complete job description was written and general objectives were clearly defined for this position. The budget included salary, travel, and necessary materials. The purpose of this unique arrangement was to bring training closer to the local church. Also, as director of evangelism, I could concentrate my efforts on smaller congregations, especially those which had greater potential for growth.

Principle #4: Churches grow when there is a favorable transition of pastors

At this point, I made the transition into this newly created ministry and began working with selected churches within the Episcopal district. Anchorage, the largest city in the state of Alaska, was experiencing exceptional growth. I traveled to Alaska to initiate a demographic study to determine if it was feasible to plant a second church in the city. The results of this study indicated that a new church planted in a different area of the city would serve a different population. The demographic study provided substantial information concerning population density and age groupings in different areas of the community.

During the following week, I conducted several teaching sessions emphasizing church planting. Armed with this information, Rev. Jesse Wilson, an associate minister at First Church, approached the pastor/presiding elder with the idea of starting a mission. Not only did the presiding elder approve of the idea, he also offered encouragement and assistance in this venture.

Rev. Wilson was instructed to proceed in planting a new church. Presiding Elder Johnson, who was also the pastor of First Church and the Episcopal Director of Evangelism, conducted the organizational meeting of the new church. The name "Church Of The Redeemed" was agreed upon by the 23 founding members. Rev. Tijuana Wilson, the wife of the founding pastor, is presently the pastor.

The question may be asked, "What were the contributing factors which made this a successful church planting venture?" We can readily see four primary factors which ensured the success of this undertaking. The first thing Rev. Wilson and his wife did was to go into serious concerted prayer asking God's direction in this venture. The second factor in planning was to assemble a core group to begin a home Bible Study. This Bible Study met in Rev. Wilson's home for a period of three months before considering organizing a church. The third factor in planning was utilizing my expertise as Episcopal Director of Evangelism with experience in church development, organization, and leadership development, to equip a core group to take on this challenge. The fourth factor in planning was doing an extensive demographic study of the Anchorage community. Today, this is a thriving congregation in the city of Anchorage, Alaska.

EXERCISE

There are three factors which facilitated growth of Amos Temple Church. Briefly explain how each of these factors made an impact on the development of this congregation.

Creating New Ministries

_____

_____

_____

_____

Adding To Pastoral Staff

_____

_____

_____

_____

Improving the Appearance of the Facility

_____

_____

_____

_____

Chapter 6

SOCIAL MINISTRIES IN ACTION

Principle # 7: Churches grow as they participate in the social arena and form good relationships with city officials and local residents

Jesus replied, "Go back and report to John what you hear and see; the blind receive sight, the lame walk, those who have leprosy are cleansed, the deaf hear, the dead are raised, and the good news is proclaimed to the poor" (Matthew 11:4–5, NIV).

"The Spirit of the Lord is upon me, because he has anointed me to preach good news to the poor. He has sent me to proclaim freedom for the prisoners, and recovery of sight to the blind, to set the oppressed free, to proclaim the year of the Lord's favor" (Luke 4:18–19).

If we are to understand and obey the mission of the church as stated by Jesus in Matthew 28:19–20, we must reach out and spread the gospel to those outside the church. Evangelism rests upon the assumption that man is lost and must be saved through the power of the Gospel. Jesus states in Luke 19:10, "For the son of man is come to seek and to save that which is lost." If the church is to be effective in meeting the spiritual, physical, and emotional needs of people, it depends on how well the message of Jesus is presented. When the Good News is presented, it must be communicated in such a way that it is understood and accepted by the unchurched or unsaved in our communities.

As we become disciples of Christ, our whole lifestyle of service and ministry changes. Then we begin to feed the hungry, clothe the naked, and visit the sick and those who are imprisoned. Looking at our communities today, it appears that we are not reaching this population.

I'm reminded of a cartoon which depicted a captain standing on the bow as the rest of the ship was below the water. He uttered the command, "Full speed ahead!" Could it be that we are not aware of the changes that have taken place in our society today? The American society has changed drastically in the last 40 years. Whether we describe these changes as "postmodern" or any other description, the changes are real.

People's values and worldviews today have undergone radical changes, and that presents a challenge to the church. When the church reaches out to postmoderns today, that is, if they reach out at all, it must convince them that the church offers real solutions to life's problems. To accomplish its mission, it must overcome some serious problems. The number-one problem is that the church as an institution is more resistant to change than other institutions in our society. Too often the church operates on the seven last words, "We've never done it this way before."

Another problem the church must overcome is the lack of effective communication. We must learn to speak the language in such a way that the unchurched can understand. Christians usually communicate in terms of what I refer to as "Holy Talk." Non-Christians, or the unchurched, do not communicate in these terms or understand the language of church folk.

The techniques and methods employed to reach the unchurched today are not very effective in this postmodern society. George Barna, a researcher, uses the word "marketing" for this process, which I feel is closely related to the word "evangelism." As the church learns where people are hurting, it must create ministries that will alleviate some of their pain. This is evangelism at its best. Churches must have an effective evangelistic program which makes use of up-to-date marketing techniques. Even though marketing is a secular term, churches have always used marketing principles. The church must make a serious effort to know where people are and what their felt needs are. Unfortunately, too many churches today are not up-to-date concerning modern or contemporary methods of reaching the lost.

Principle #2: Churches grow when evangelism is one of the highest priorities of ministry

The church needs to fulfill the cultural mandate it has to move out into the world. McGavran says, "The masses are learning that they do not have to live in perpetual poverty, because educated men inform the poor that they have the right to plenty and organize and arm them to wrench a share of this world's goods from the privileged."

Peter Wagner, a protégé of McGavran, follows with this commentary: "Matters having to do with the poor and oppressed, with justice and peace, with brotherhood and liberation, with wealth and lifestyle, with discipleship and the kingdom of God is all part of the concern of biblical Christians."

If the church is to achieve these lofty goals of the cultural mandate, two general types of ministry must be utilized, namely social service and social action. To this end, many churches and denominations have established social concerns departments. There may be some confusion or misunderstanding as it relates to the social mandate. I believe a brief discussion of these items is in order.

Social service is a ministry geared to meet the needs of individuals and groups in a direct and immediate way. When a catastrophic event happens, social service will provide food, clothing, shelter, medical supplies, and whatever other needs are deemed as necessary. The energy of most churches has been focused more often on social service, such as benevolence or a food ministry.

Social action is a ministry geared toward changing social structures. It responds to causes on a much higher level and its effect is more far-reaching than just administering food programs. The Civil Rights Movement is a classic example of churches being engaged in social action. Another prime example is the Hope in Youth initiative in the city of Los Angeles which mobilized more than 200 churches by the four affiliates of the Industrial Areas Foundation. Fundamental churches usually referred to as evangelical put greater emphasis on salvation, at the same time maintaining a certain indifference toward social service or social action.

I, as the Episcopal director, was introduced to the Industrial Areas Foundation (IAF) by Larry McNeil who was a member of the IAF staff. McNeil was the field supervisor for the State of California. The South Central Organizing Committee (SCOC) was one of 23 affiliates of the national body. The Industrial Areas Foundation was founded by Saul Alinsky. These affiliate organizations concentrated on forming partnerships with school systems and trained community leaders in parenting, leadership, and empowerment.

The Olympics were staged in Los Angeles during the '80s. Politicians and civic leaders were convinced that the city would go deeply in the red. Therefore, they enlisted thousands of volunteers who worked tirelessly to make sure Los Angeles would host this international event adequately. As a result, the Olympic Committee had a windfall profit of $280 million dollars. Our research indicated that there were no plans for how this money would be distributed or used. It was only natural that SCOC and the three other affiliates of the IAF would proceed to assist them in determining where to spend some of this money. Therefore, the four affiliate community organizations were of the opinion that a substantial amount of this money should be granted to community organizations of the city. Dr. William R. Johnson and I, who had undergone extensive training in leadership and community organizing through the IAF, were leaders in SCOC.

I asked Ms. Toni Jackson-Williams to write a proposal for the amount of $70,000 for the creation of a Volley Ball League

SOCIAL MINISTRIES IN ACTION 109

composed of churches in the city of Riverside, California. This proposal served as a model for 26 other community entities. The proposals were ultimately packaged into one master proposal, which was ultimately submitted to the Olympic Committee. During the next two months, the four local affiliates of the Industrial Areas Foundation combined to conduct a campaign to ensure that an amount of 2 million dollars would be allotted to these 26 community entities and administrated by directors representing the four Industrial Areas Foundation affiliate organizations. I, as one of the leaders of the South Central Organizing Committee, was assigned as director of the South Central area of Los Angeles.

During the next few months, many one-on-one meetings were held with city officials, political leaders, the media, and officials of the Olympic Committee. The purpose of meeting with the Olympic Committee was to discuss in person the rationale for the amount of money we were asking for in our proposal. One major event was held at one of the city parks in Los Angeles. It was estimated that approximately 3,000 persons attended. The event was well covered by news media, political officials, and three television stations. As a result of the ongoing events, the four IAF affiliates were awarded a grant of 3½ million dollars for the 26 community organizations.

The Olympic Archery event was held in the Riverside area; therefore, the community was eligible for a portion of the Olympic funds. I, as pastor of Amos Temple Church, seized this opportunity and instructed my grant writer, Ms. Toni Jackson-Williams, to write a proposal for a citywide volleyball league among several churches of the Riverside area. This resulted in a $70,000 grant to organize and administer the league.

The California Minimum Wage

The four Los Angeles affiliates of the Industrial Areas Foundation began to work on another project which may be considered another level of social ministry. The rationale for this approach is that it makes more sense to teach a man to fish instead of just giving him a fish every day. These affiliated churches decided that the minimum wage must be raised to $4.05 an hour in California. Dr. William Johnson and I, both of whom had undergone extensive training in leadership and community organizing, played a critical leadership role in this project. The research arm of the organization provided us with significant bits of information regarding the minimum wage.

In California, the minimum wage is not raised by the state legislature. Instead, there is a five-member commission, composed of two members representing the business community, two members representing labor, and one member that is neutral, known as the Industrial Welfare Commission, that is charged to make a determination of what the minimum wage will be in the state. Having been privy to this information, our lobbying efforts were focused on the neutral representative on the commission.

It took 18 months of negotiations with the media, politicians, and organizing public actions to bring this issue of need to the public. On the date that the commission was meeting in San Francisco, 11 50-passenger buses were chartered to carry 500 people to San Francisco to be present at this vitally important meeting of the commission. These 500 people, who had traveled from Los Angeles on the big yellow school buses, sat quietly in prayer as the panel members were being instructed to answer "Aye" or "Nay" when their names were called. It was a tense moment as the count was tied with two ayes and two nays.

The fifth panelist's name was finally called, and she answered with a strong, audible, "Aye." The whole contingent of 500 onlookers immediately broke out in a loud victory celebration. Finally, through this ministry of social action, the minimum wage was raised in California for the first time in almost ten years.

As time passed, I maintained contact with most of the churches in the Episcopal district. Instruments were designed to evaluate the progress and activity of the churches in the district. Churches were now showing positive results in both quantitative and qualitative growth. Positive effects were realized in areas of evangelism, vision, administration, and church development in churches which were serviced by this ministry. There were many successes and accomplishments, and also some failures. I am convinced that things don't "just happen." God has his own purposes, even if we don't always understand, and in time, God will reveal his purposes to us.

The pastor of a church in Richmond, California, suffered a fatal heart attack within four weeks after he was assigned to this charge. This was a painful loss to the church as the ministry seemed to be progressing very well. I was asked by the bishop if I would consider filling in for a period of three months until a replacement could be found. I agreed to do so, knowing that it was only for a period of three months. I looked at it as a positive experience of serving in another conference. The only unfavorable aspect of this arrangement was that the three months was extended to six years. However, there are no accidents in God's economy. It wasn't obvious to me at this time, but the move to the Northern California area offered different opportunities in ministry.

The presiding bishop, Episcopal director, and the administrative assistant arrived at the San Francisco Airport at about 9:15 A.M. Saturday morning. The purpose of this trip was to introduce me to the congregation as the interim pastor. It was convenient to take BART (Bay Area Rapid Transit District), an efficient rail transportation system serving several cities in the East Bay. This was a rare experience traveling through a tunnel on the bottom of the ocean to reach our destination in approximately 25 minutes. Several officers of Davis Chapel Church were anxiously waiting to meet us at the BART station in Richmond.

We were taken to the hotel where overnight accommodations had been arranged. Later in the evening, we met with a representative group of officers who gave us a report on the state of the church. I was happy to learn that the affairs of the church were in excellent condition. As the bishop introduced me to these officers, he assured them that this was just an interim assignment for approximately three months.

On Sunday morning, we arrived at the church at about 10 A.M. I was presented to the congregation as an interim pastor. The service proved to be exhilarating and spirit filled. The gospel choir's rendition of music was uplifting and added much to the service. After all preliminaries of the service were taken care of, the bishop presented me as the pastor. He had not indicated that I would bring the message at this service, but I knew that I should be prepared. One of the auxiliaries of the church had prepared a repast after the service, which presented an opportunity for members to become acquainted with their interim pastor.

The next weekend, the officers of the church and I did a thorough assessment of the community, including a visit to the hospital. One of the first persons visited in the hospital was Ms. Corrine Phelps. There was no way of knowing at this time that she would play a consequential role in bringing people to Christ and joining the church.

Possibility Thinking

At one time, the area was a very desirable middle-class area, but as people experienced "redemption and lift," they relocated to more desirable areas. This accounted for the fact that most of the members lived in other parts of the city and only came back to the North Richmond area to worship on Sundays. As the members traveled the streets of North Richmond coming to worship, it seemed as if they were oblivious to their surroundings. They were not aware of the general appearance of the community.

As we continued on our tour, we noticed small groups of people on certain street corners engaged in some type of "transactions." I learned later that these individuals were staking out their territory to sell drugs.

In other sections of the community we observed scantily clad young ladies seemingly aimlessly walking the streets. To add to the situation, I was informed that Richmond had the dubious distinction of having the highest homicide rate of any city its size in the United States. Instead of seeing this as an almost impossible situation, I perceived it as an opportunity to be creative in developing ministries which would meet the needs of this community. Robert Schuller, the founder and pastor of the Crystal Cathedral in Orange County, California, had positively influenced my thinking in the area of church growth and development. In one of his books he talks about "Possibility Thinking." He also coined the phrase, "Find a need and fill it." It is a fact that there are always possibilities in any situation one is confronted with.

As I studied the situation I came to the conclusion that I had a choice of two options which I could pursue.

(1) I could move the church to a different location in the city which was more conducive for attracting new members to the church.
(2) I could change the worship service which would be more appealing to the residents in this area of the city.

After carefully considering these options, I decided that I would not move the church to another area. My priority would be to make the necessary changes in our worship service and add ministries that meet the people's needs.

As time passed, we noticed that visitors began to visit the church on a consistent basis, and many of them united with the church. Now, we were not naïve enough to believe that they were visiting the church because of something we were doing. Most likely people were coming to see and check out the new pastor in town and perhaps they were curious about how the church was adjusting to the loss of their regular pastor. I wasn't so much concerned about these reasons, I was more concerned about creating a worship service which was uplifting and delivering sermons which would touch their heartfelt needs.

When many of these persons walked down the aisle to unite with the church, they were informed that they would be required to attend the new member classes before they would be granted full membership in the church. A church growth principle states that churches grow when new ministries that meet needs are added. With this influx of new members, it was necessary to prepare new member materials for instruction concerning the doctrine, history, and administrative structure of the church.

The first new member class was taught after the first month of my assignment. Nine new members completed this course which was labeled "Discipleship 101." Later, these new members stood before the congregation and were administered the ritual of Confirmation and Reception into the Church.

Almost four months had passed since I was assigned to this church and since I was only an interim pastor, I assumed I would be relieved of this assignment at the winter meeting. At this meeting when asked to report on the ministry of the Davis Chapel, I stated that the church had met all of its responsibilities. I further stated that the congregation was well on the way of healing after the tragic loss of their regular pastor.

Although I waited to hear who would relieve me as the regular pastor of Davis Chapel Church, it simply did not happen. At that meeting, the bishop stated that I would remain as interim pastor at Davis Chapel. I wondered if I heard him correctly when he made that announcement.

After the meeting adjourned, I hurried to the bishop's office to remind him of his promise to bring me back to the Southern California Conference. The bishop answered rather sheepishly that he had received several petitions and requests that the interim pastor would be assigned as the regular pastor. After recuperating from the shock of hearing those words, I began to formulate a vision for this church. This was the beginning of a tenure of six exciting years of ministry in the Bay Area of California.

The officers requested a meeting with me as quickly as possible to plan for my travel, lodging, and salary. It was agreed that other less pressing details could be taken care of at a later date. A breakfast meeting took place at a convenient restaurant on the first Monday after the closing of the conference. After opening the meeting with a prayer, an interesting statement was made by the chairman of the board. "Pastor, just do what we tell you, and we will take good care of you." I didn't respond to the statement at this time, but I knew that this could be an administrative problem later. This working breakfast turned out to be a very good session as all of the items on the agenda were covered.

Visitors continued to visit our worship services. We still exceeded the 30 percent rule of visitors uniting with the church. Among the visitors was County Supervisor Powell who visited several times over a period of a year. Two city councilmen were also consistent visitors to our worship services. Eventually the city council commissioned me as the drug commissioner for the city. This presented a wonderful opportunity to develop a social ministry as there were many needs in this community.

My first venture in this position was attending a town hall meeting. As I arose to contribute to the discussions at hand, the person in charge immediately made this statement. "Sit down, Reverend. You preachers always want to take over in our meetings." This statement was made with such an air of authority that I proceeded to take my seat. Wisdom dictated that I would need to sit quietly and observe the proceedings of the meeting.

To be effective in this position, I began to explore a more creative way to introduce myself to this community. It dawned on me that I hadn't prayed for God's guidance when I accepted this position. I did feel a certain amount of guilt as I had always encouraged my parishioners to develop a strong prayer life as they faced challenges in their lives.

During the next week, I set aside a half hour at noon each day to pray specifically for God's guidance in this position. God does answer prayer, and he answers in ways that we least expect. One afternoon a small group of musicians had a jam session directly across the street from the parsonage. They were sounding pretty good, so I went over and introduced myself and let them know that I appreciated their music. They informed me that they were not really an organized group, but they enjoyed getting together and just have fun playing together. I informed them that I had something in mind that may be of interest to them, and that it would take some time to work out details of what I had in mind. I told them that I would contact them later regarding this plan.

The musicians showed an interest in what I had said, even though I hadn't said very much.

The first person I needed to contact was Ms. Corinne Phelps, who had a good relationship with most of the residents in North Richmond. She was just the one who could help me work this plan that I had in mind. I told her my plan was to have a block party on a Saturday afternoon. Corinne informed me that she knew a person who had a 40-foot flatbed trailer and maybe we could convince him to bring his trailer and set it up in the intersection. Next, it was necessary to clear this idea through City Hall.

This request was granted, and we were issued a permit by the city to block off an intersection for a period of four hours. We decided that this was not to be a fund-raising event; it was organized as a public relations event to promote goodwill between all age groups. Corinne insisted that I should meet some of the gang members and "local entrepreneurs" who were vending their "products" in certain choice locations of the community. Her suggestion didn't appeal to me, as I was uncomfortable with the idea. I never gave her a direct answer to her request. Yet she was extremely persistent in promoting this idea.

One morning about 10 o'clock, Corrine called me and told me to be ready in half an hour because a group of fellows were waiting on me to come and talk with them. There was no way I could get out of this so I agreed to meet with this group. Corrine picked me up, and we headed to the location where the group was waiting.

As we approached the designated site, the group stood on the curb in a straight line. I had no idea why they lined up in this manner. My speech was very brief and simple. I stated that I was the new pastor in town, and that I was also appointed drug commissioner for the city. One person eventually spoke up and asked if there was going to be a block party in the neighborhood soon. We let them know that we were in the process of making plans for this at this particular time. Their response was that they would like to be involved, and they would make sure that nothing would "go down" at this event.

On the way back to my residence, I asked Corrine why these young men lined up on the curb when we arrived to talk to them. She explained this was a procedure that the police required when they came into the neighborhood to question these men about some problem.

As planned, early on the day of the event, the owner of the flatbed trailer maneuvered it in its designated place in the intersection. A few of the young men arrived and began to assist me in bringing out folding chairs and running a power line from my residence to provide power for the musicians. To my surprise, a couple of vending trucks were stationed in a convenient location to provide hot dogs and hamburgers and other refreshments.

The musicians were in rare form that day. There was much dancing, and from time to time, people would show their talents by volunteering to sing accompanied by the musicians. People in the neighborhood brought tables and played dominoes and checkers. Others just sat around and enjoyed the entertainment.

To my surprise, the person who had suggested that I take my seat in the town hall meeting arrived at this event. He asked if I was raising money for my church by this event. I informed him that this was not an event to raise money; it was just a way to do something for the neighborhood. As he walked away, he mumbled, "This is a good thing."

Who were the people who had come to enjoy this event? There were members of various churches, drug pushers, gang members, and just ordinary people. There were no incidents such as fights, arguments, or shootings. This turned out to be quite a festive celebration. We were successful in improving our relationship with the community, and this is what we set out to accomplish.

What was the growth principle behind this accomplishment?

When we meet situations in our lives that we don't have the answers to, God will provide resources to help us accomplish our goals. I recall an old familiar adage, "He might not come when you want him to, but he always comes on time." Recall in the book of Exodus 17:11-13, as Israel fought its first battle against the Amalekites, as long as Moses held up his rod the Israelites would win. When Moses grew weary, Aaron and Hur held up his arms.

Ms. Phelps, who was well thought of in the North Richmond community, used her influence to get people involved in this event. She was effective in publicizing this event throughout the community by word of mouth. She definitely had the gift of evangelism, as she was responsible for many members joining the church. This was verified when she attended the Spiritual Gifts seminar and took the Spiritual Gifts Inventory. Her two highest scoring areas on the inventory were Evangelism and Intercessory Prayer. She had this uncanny ability to communicate with all classes of people. Her faith had helped her to overcome so many tragedies in her life, such as losing her two sons in drive-by shootings.

Principle #2: Churches grow when evangelism is the highest priority of ministry

The success of the block party had a significant effect on the ministry of Davis Chapel. I began to walk the streets of the community and engage many of the young people on the streets in conversation. This became a routine, and they began to refer to me as their pastor, even though they were not attending church.

One Monday morning as I arrived at the church at about 9:30 A.M., there was a person parked near the entrance of my office. He stated that he would like to discuss a matter with me. To my great surprise this was the same brother, Bubba, who had "invited" me to "sit down" at the town hall meeting, and who had also attended the block party. I invited him up to my office, but he stated that he would rather talk with me outside.

He informed me that there were serious instances of abuse by the police in this community. He described many of these incidents vividly at length. They had been trying to solve these problems, but only minimum progress was being made. Bubba finally came directly to the point of his visit when he asked if there was anything I could do in helping them solve these problems. Some ideas were beginning to enter my mind, although I decided not to share them at this particular time. Instead, I said, "Yes, I think there may be something we could do together to alleviate some of these problems. If you are available Wednesday morning,

I would like to discuss this idea at a breakfast meeting."

He stated, "I think that is a great idea, Pastor, and I will even pay for the breakfast." At this point, a positive relationship of trust was being formed which is necessary to create a positive atmosphere to work with all aspects of the community.

We both arrived at the restaurant at the designated time and after we were seated, we engaged in some small talk, which had nothing to do with why we were meeting. Finally, Bubba began to explain why he wanted to meet with me. He stated that he had been working with the youth of the community, helping them to stay out of trouble and encouraging them to stay in school and learn some type of trade. He told me how the police were using excessive force when making arrests. They would even plant drugs on the young men as they were arrested.

I was surprised to learn that there were no other pastors involved with these issues in North Richmond. In fact, one pastor warned me that I would be exposing myself to grave danger if I were walking the streets alone in certain areas of this community. One or two young men would always walk with me when I was out in the community. I learned later that Bubba had arranged for people to accompany me each morning to make sure that no one would harm me. These walks provided an opportunity to learn more about the community. These young men, and sometimes young women, were comfortable in sharing because trust had been established. They would freely share information about the community.

I learned so much about the drug trade and how it was organized and distributed. Eventually I became knowledgeable of who killed who and even who would be killed later. As time passed, I began to realize I was putting myself in danger as I was privy to too much information of this type. I realized that if something "went down" and I knew who the principals were, a "contract" could be put out on me!

Bubba informed me that he had been attempting to get the chief of police, the county sheriff, and other city and county officials to attend the town hall meetings. Obviously none of these officials could arrange their busy schedules to attend these meetings. Bubba suggested that perhaps my position as drug commissioner for the city could influence the county and city officials to attend these community meetings. We were so excited about these prospects that we established a tentative date for this event. We agreed that I would contact the city and county officials and at the same time inform them that we would expect them to arrange their schedules to attend a town hall meeting. Ms. Phelps and Bubba accepted the responsibility for advertising this event. We had a window of two weeks to take care of all of these arrangements.

On the evening of the event we made several assignments. Ushers from Davis Chapel volunteered their services to assist during the meeting. An unofficial security group was organized to stay outside to observe anything that might interrupt the meeting. As our guests arrived, they would be ushered to a room where they would receive a briefing of the plans for this meeting. At this point, I left Ms. Phelps and Bubba to finish the briefing. By this time, the auditorium was almost filled to capacity. I had stationed myself at the door where I could greet each person as they arrived.

One young man, more than 6½ feet tall with dreadlocks, began to engage me in conversation. I noticed that he was very articulate and expressed himself well. Before the meeting started, I spoke to the audience and explained certain rules that must be obeyed. Number one, no profanity will be tolerated at this meeting. Number two, persons will speak only when they are recognized to do so. A maximum of three minutes will be allotted for each speaker. I reminded them that I was one of the smallest people in the room and I realize that I could not make anyone do anything that they didn't want to do. But there is one option that I could and would exercise. I would declare an end to the meeting if it got out of control. The meeting proceeded very well as everyone abided by the rules which were explained to them.

The exchange of ideas and concerns in the meeting served to enlighten the city officials, law enforcement representatives, and residents of the community. It was suggested that this type of meeting should be held periodically. The officials committed to this idea also.

After the meeting was officially closed, I noticed that this young man that I had talked to earlier wanted to further our conversation. He informed me that he was a law student from Yale University and had come to San Francisco as an intern with a law firm. He further stated that he would like to work with the community as his project. And so he did.

Greater Richmond Interfaith Program

Principle #7: Churches grow as they participate in the social arena

Davis Chapel was a member of a nonprofit organization called GRIP (Greater Richmond Interfaith Program). Rev. Herman C. Riley, a pastor of Davis Chapel in the late '70s, was one of the founders of GRIP. This organization was formed by a group of churches to combat racial strife in the city. A group of officers from GRIP came to the church to encourage me as the new pastor to become active again in this organization. These officers thoroughly explained the history, purpose, and activities of the organization. It currently has about 28 churches as members of the organization. Davis Chapel's membership was reactivated immediately.

After a year and a half of serving on the board of directors, I was elected and installed as chairman of the board. GRIP receives much of its operating budget from the Catholic Charities Foundation. Some of its programs are an adult day care center, Project Home Again, and a summer leadership development program for high school students. During the last year of my tenure as pastor of Davis Chapel, Mr. John Olmsted, the president of Volunteers of America, came to my office to discuss a proposal.

This nonprofit agency had been operating a free lunch kitchen known as the Super Center. This kitchen served approximately 250 hot lunches daily, Monday through Friday. The Volunteers of America had operated this program for several years and now wanted to turn this program over to GRIP. Mr. Olmsted stated that if we were interested, they would deed the facility to GRIP at no charge. This facility was equipped with a commercial kitchen, with all necessary appliances, and a spacious dining area. GRIP identified this ministry as a community need; therefore, we accepted the responsibility of operating this feeding program.

Project Home Again

Principle #6: Churches grow as they create ministries that meet the needs of the target audience. The use of marketing techniques will aid in determining the needs of the community.

The city of Richmond had an unusually high population of homeless persons. As the chairman of the board of GRIP, I explored ideas about how we could find solutions to the homeless problem. We learned that it was not difficult to get fairly accurate statistics of the homeless population in the community. We realized that just getting the numbers would not give us an adequate picture of the average homeless person, however. Therefore, we decided to go into the community and interview a sample of homeless people to determine why they became a part of the homeless population. The results of these interviews revealed that loss of jobs was one of the root causes of the high incidence of homelessness in the community. Armed with this information, we were able to begin formulating a plan to assist homeless people in restoring their dignity and becoming productive citizens again.

One of our first steps in organizing was to pair an affluent suburban congregation with an inner-city congregation. Initially, there were six inner-city churches and six suburban churches. This made a total of 12 churches participating in this ministry. We wanted to see how well this paired unit met the goals which had been established. Three members from each of the paired churches were selected as a joint committee to coordinate the ministry between them. This committee would interview a particular homeless person in order to determine whether this individual would be a good prospect for success in this ministry. These interviews provided certain background information such as educational level, skills possessed, dependent children, and marital status. At this point, the committee would dismiss the person but instruct him\her to meet with them at a future time. In the meantime, the committee would discuss among themselves whether this person would be a good prospect for rehabilitating.

Davis Chapel and its partner church were designated to run a pilot program to work out any unforeseen problems or glitches. Three homeless persons were recommended to us to interview. We proceeded to interview them, and finally chose a young lady by the name of Charlene. Charlene was a high school graduate, single, with one child. We were impressed with the confidence she showed in the interviewing process. She stated that she had lost her job as a waitress about three months ago. As a result, she was not able to maintain her apartment or pay her car note; therefore, it was repossessed.

The suburban church coordinator set her up with an adequate living environment. Charlene took the initiative and soon found a job. Again, Ms. Busic, the coordinator of our suburban church, stepped in and provided Charlene with a dependable automobile so that it would be more convenient for her to work and attend school. The committee assisted Charlene in enrolling in the community college to pursue a course leading to a career in nursing. Both churches were briefed by their representatives on a routine basis and were impressed with the success of the ministry.

GRIP notified our committee we were to meet with the board of directors for the purpose of evaluating the effectiveness of this pilot program. The committee met and began to prepare the report with confidence that GRIP would officially bring on other paired churches. The Project Home Again ministry offered a unique approach to the homeless problem. This was an ideal time for Charlene to be introduced to the board of directors. Things were going unusually well. Charlene was now employed, living in her own apartment, attending community college, and maintaining a 3.5 GPA.

On a Tuesday morning my office received a call from Seattle, Washington. The voice identified herself as Charlene and began to explain her situation, or perhaps I should say, her predicament. It was shocking to accept or believe the voice on the other end of the phone was Charlene. Panic began to set in as many things began running through my mind. Many hours had been spent getting this ministry up and running. Was all of this for naught? Had we done an adequate job of checking Charlene's background and character? Had we made our selection too hastily? What effect would this have on the Home Again Project?

Charlene informed me that a warrant was out on her and that she had been extradited back to Seattle and was in jail. I was able to secure two official phone numbers to call for more details regarding this case. Ms. Busic, the coordinator in my partnered church, was immediately informed of this pressing event and within an hour we met to discuss this problem. With these phone numbers, Ms. Busic was able to contact the prosecutor and judge and ask that Charlene's arraignment be the last case on the docket on Wednesday. This request was granted. Ms. Busic immediately made reservations on a 6 A.M. flight from Oakland to Seattle, with a return flight from Seattle to Oakland at 11 P.M.

Ms. Busic arrived in Seattle as planned and went directly to the district attorney's office. Apparently she was able to speak with the district attorney, but I am unaware of what transpired at this point. I do know that the judge dropped all charges at Charlene's arraignment Thursday. Ms. Busic and Charlene were back in the Oakland area around 2 A.M. Thursday.

On Friday noon, the joint committee met and later Charlene was introduced to the board of directors of GRIP. The executive director received the report of this ministry, orally, and then a written document. GRIP decided to arrange teaching sessions for the other four paired churches before activating the Project Home Again ministry. Charlene finished her nursing course and is employed at a hospital in the Bay Area. She is also in college preparing for a RN certification.

Advocacy Ministry

Principle # 7: Churches grow as they participate in the social arena

A committee representing the juvenile court, Richmond Unified School District, and the Greater Richmond Interfaith Program were meeting for the purpose of writing a proposal to submit to the State of California. As chairperson of the board of GRIP, I represented this nonprofit agency, which will be further discussed later.

After this meeting, the public defender approached me and through our conversation, I was apprised of some of the problems the public defender was facing in his work. He revealed many of his concerns of how the juvenile court system was not always operating in the best interests of the juveniles. For instance, he related that he only had about five to seven minutes to talk to his clients before their case was called. We both agreed that we would organize a group of seniors who would be willing to stand with these juveniles when their cases were called.

When the judge noticed there was an adult standing with a youth, it seemed that the attitudes of the judge and prosecutor would change. It was apparent that when a senior stood next to a juvenile in court, the judges' decisions were less harsh. In fact, many of the judges' decisions were extremely lenient.

Initially, I requested a conference with the presiding judge to discuss my desire to organize an advocacy ministry which was badly needed in our community. The judge granted my request with one condition, that those who participate in this ministry must be briefed regarding rules and procedures. The judge explained that this ministry must not cause any distractions from court protocol.

There were many exciting incidents that happened over a period of time in this ministry. One incident in particular is worth mentioning. Deborah had a son, Albert, who was doing very well as an employee of American Airlines. Over a period of three years, he had never missed a day at work. His evaluations were always outstanding. It seemed as if he had a bright future with the airline.

As with most young people, he enjoy going to parties. One evening at a party, there was some type of altercation and a person was killed. In the midst of the confusion, Albert was arrested. He was eventually charged with murder, but yet he consistently insisted that he had nothing to do with this incident. There were motions for continuance offered several times during the year. In the meantime, investigations were being made by the defense lawyer. Because of my position as drug commissioner for the city, I had formed excellent relationships with all segments of the community. Because of this relationship, I usually knew who did many of the homicides. I eventually put out feelers trying to find out more information about this particular murder that took place at the party.

A few days later I got a response to my feeler. "Pastor, we don't think you should pursue this incident because it may put you in a dangerous position. The police have one of their snitches in jail who fingered Albert." I relayed this information to the defense attorney, who found that this snitch had a 25-inch color television in his cell.

At the next court hearing, the prosecuting attorney stated that they did not have enough evidence to prosecute. The judge made a simple statement, "Case dismissed." At this point, something happened in this court session that perhaps no one has ever witnessed before. The mother stood up from her seat and let out a scream, then preceded running around the whole courtroom screaming. The judge sat there transfixed in a state of confusion for a few moments and was unable to say a word. It was several minutes before he did utter the words," Order in the court." This young man was reinstated in his position with American Airlines with all back pay for a period of 18 months.

Six-County Commissioner

One day, the receptionist informed me that there was a call from County Supervisor Powell's office. In returning the call, the supervisor asked if I was available to come to his office as there was an urgent issue he would like to discuss with me. Several days later, an appointment with the supervisor took place.

After the preliminary cordial greetings, Supervisor Powell came directly to the point. He stated that a six-county commission was being formed to study the possibility of creating a regional governing body. He further stated that he had, for some time, followed my ministry, and he would like to recommend me to this commission representing Contra Costa County. Supervisor Powell continued to explain what this appointment would entail. This commission would meet for four hours each week for three years. The supervisor suggested that I take some time to consider this opportunity, although he called me just two days later for my decision. I accepted this appointment at this time. The president of the commission was a Mr. Clawson, the CEO of Bank of America, and the chancellor of the University of California, Berkeley, was the vice president.

The commission was composed of a total number of 21 members. This service of three years on this commission was a valuable growing experience for me. Even though my work on this commission wasn't directly related to ministry, the work of this commission would certainly have a positive economic effect on the lives of people residing in Contra Costa County. I was exposed to experiences which related to church administration that was of great value.

Spiritual Gifts

At this time, the growth of the church was at such a fast pace that it became difficult to assimilate all of the new members into the church. Also, the church's infrastructure was not adequately prepared to deal with the growing numbers of new members. A series of seminars were planned, such as Knowing Your Spiritual Gifts, Leadership Development, and expanding the Christian Education Curriculum. The first principle that we must understand is that the church must not be organized around the model of a dictatorship or a democracy. Several years ago I learned that the church is a theocracy. The church is usually referred to as the body of Christ which is a live organism, not an organization. God designed the church as an organism with

Christ as the head and each member functioning with a spiritual gift.

Principle #10: Spiritual gifts enhance church growth

"A spiritual gift is a special attribute given by the Holy Spirit to each member of the body of Christ according to God's grace for use within the context of the body." There are three major biblical passages relating to spiritual gifts found in the New Testament. These passages are found in Romans 12, I Corinthians 12, and Ephesians 4.

The first priority is to learn about the spiritual gifts which God has placed in the congregation. Pastor John McArthur says, "No local congregation will be what it should be, what Jesus prayed that it should be, what the Holy Spirit gifted it and empowered it to be, until it understands spiritual gifts." Therefore, a conference was arranged with Ms. Greer, the director of Christian education, to plan for a series of spiritual gifts seminars. These seminars were organized on three components: (1) learning about the gifts, (2) administering the Spiritual Gifts Inventory, and (3) an interview with each participant to assist them in understanding which ministries are compatible with their gift.

After completing the first series of Spiritual Gifts seminars, the director of Christian education approached me and informed me that she had decided to resign from the position of director of Christian Education. I was completely surprised at her decision, as she had been doing an excellent job in this position for many years. Actually, I began to panic as this came so unexpected. After a few moments, I managed to regain my composure and asked her why she decided to resign from her position. She stated, "Pastor, as you know, after completing the Spiritual Gifts seminar, I learned that my spiritual gift is evangelism. Therefore, I would like to work on the Evangelism Committee." Her request was granted on condition that she would recommend someone as her replacement. Ms. Gray stated that there was a person who had been assisting her for some time who is capable of serving as the director of Christian education. Her next request was asking if she could have the third Sunday of each month declared as Family and Friends Day. This request was also granted.

On the next third Sunday, people were filing into the church before the 11 A.M. service was scheduled to start. The sanctuary was completely filled when the worship began; others were directed to the balcony. During the worship, there seemed to be an air of excitement and enthusiasm. Families and friends were recognized during the service, and this was quite exciting. After the sermon, an invitation to unite with the church was extended, and to my surprise, 14 people came forward to unite with the church. It was apparent that much planning had gone into the preparation for this day. Everyone was invited to the Fellowship Hall for dinner after service. This event was so successful that it became a tradition that was repeated three times during the year. This venture was a prime example how spiritual gifts enhances the growth of the church.

Parenting Training By Lily Foundation

Several years ago, the Lily Foundation sponsored a three-year program to certify people to teach parenting. After hearing about this program, I immediately contacted the General Secretary of Christian Education and inquired if it was possible to be recommended to participate in this program. I explained to the general secretary that I had unique problems in my church as many of our teenage girls were becoming mothers. Therefore, we faced an urgent need to teach parenting skills. The general secretary informed me that they already had their quota, but he would see if there was any way that people from Davis Chapel could be included in this valuable training.

Several days later, he called and informed me that he had found additional funding from the AFL-CIO Labor Union for three other positions. Two members of Davis Chapel and I were selected to participate in this ministry. After finishing the three-year program, all the participants received an official certificate certifying them to teach parenting skills. Of course, we were asked to make a commitment to teach three complete sessions of this 13-week program. The director of the program also suggested that we could fulfill this requirement by teaching parenting at churches or various boys and girls clubs. Often, children are placed in foster homes. Some social service agencies accept these classes, taught by individuals certified to teach parenting, as a requirement for mothers to regain custody of their children from foster care.

In the meantime, the number of pregnant teenagers continued to grow. I really didn't have an answer to this problem. A meeting with the prayer committee was convened. I asked if they would pray with me concerning this problem. We arranged to pray at a designated time each day, asking God to give us direction in dealing with this problem.

Two weeks later, at the 11 o'clock service, a lady walked down the aisle to unite with the church. It was my practice to ask those who come forth to make a decision to unite with the church if they would like to make a statement. She indicated that she was the director of a family agency downtown. As I listened to her statement I found it extremely difficult to restrain myself. Without even giving any thought as to how I would respond to her statement, I simply said, "God sent you."

During the next week I arranged a conference with her to discuss the possibility of initiating parenting classes. At this meeting, she volunteered to set up and teach the parenting classes. She even stated that she would provide the materials for the class without any cost to the church. The initial class was not only composed of teenage mothers, but many grandmothers also enrolled in the class. This was understandable as many of the mothers were on drugs, so it became necessary for grandmothers to assume the responsibility of raising their grandchildren. We are living in a postmodern society today where many changes are taking place in values, mores, and methods of parenting.

The three basic institutions, the home, church, and school, which in past years were the stabilizing factors sustaining society, have been adversely affected by these changing attitudes and values, especially regarding child rearing. It is natural that grandmothers would seek help in caring for their grandchildren. Establishing this new ministry of parenting fulfilled a need.

Housing

As we surveyed the community, we noted that there were a large number of vacant lots and houses that were not occupied. We established an unofficial committee of persons living in the community of North Richmond to discuss and explore solutions to these problems. After several meetings of this committee, we decided to focus on remodeling these houses. Our research indicated that these houses and lots had reverted to the county or the city of Richmond because of unpaid taxes. After lengthy discussions, we decided that we would form a nonprofit housing corporation. Since the idea originated in Davis Chapel, four of the seven elected board members were members of Davis Chapel.

We completed the application to form this nonprofit and forward it to Sacramento, the capital of California. We were eventually approved as a 501(c)(3) nonprofit entity for building and remodeling homes. We were now in position to transact business with the city of Richmond and county of Contra Costa and meet the needs of citizens in the city and county.

Tutorial Program Fulfills Community Needs

The California annual conference convened in August 1992, and I was anticipating returning to Southern California. In a conference with the bishop, I requested to be transferred back to the Southern California Conference. The bishop assured me that I would be transferred back to the Los Angeles area. Therefore, I had made all necessary arrangements to relocate to the Southern California area.

The following week, the Southern California Annual Conference convened. My transfer was accepted. I was assigned as pastor of Calvary CME Church located in Pasadena, California. Even though this turned out to be a tenure of only one year, significant accomplishments were realized during this time.

I submitted a proposal to the city of Pasadena for a tutorial program. Calvary CME Church was granted $60,000 for this project. An organization of home teachers would meet with their classes for three hours each Friday morning in Calvary's Fellowship Hall to teach science. We received permission from the city of Pasadena to block off the streets for a block party. This turned out to be quite a gala event with music and dancing in the streets. People set up booths on the church parking lot selling their merchandise. Opening our church facilities for such events created positive attitudes toward the church in the minds of the residents of the community. This resulted in many members of the community uniting with Calvary.

The Hope in Youth Initiative

During this period, I was actively involved with the Southern California Organizing Committee (SCOC), one of the four local affiliates of the Industrial Areas Foundation. The main focus of this organization is to empower people to better their lives through social action. The IAF teaches "Never do for people what they can do for themselves." Another way of saying this is, instead of giving a person a fish, it is better to teach them how to fish. Some things may be done more effectively when it is done by working together cooperatively.

The challenge before us at this time was to secure funding for the newly proposed Hope in Youth Initiative. During the year, the four affiliates worked together as a highly organized unit. Several major actions (rallies) were successfully staged with as many as 4,000 people attending. These events were covered very well by the media, newspapers, and television. As expected, many politicians attended these actions with a minimum amount of coercing.

One of our most significant events was held at Phillips Temple Church where almost 1,000 people gathered. The mayor of Los Angeles was also in attendance. The highlight of this meeting was that the mayor committed to add a line item in the city budget of $3 million for the Hope in Youth Initiative. This item was eventually approved by the city council.

We were now assured of $5 million funding for this initiative, $3 million from the city of Los Angeles, and $2 million from the United States government. The prayer committees of each affiliate were constantly engaged in prayer during the entire period of negotiations for the Hope in Youth Initiative. The funding from the county was crucial as the proposals were written for a total amount of $8 million. Without the $3 million from the county, the proposal would have to be rewritten and revised to operate only on the $5 million that we were assured of.

Leaders from the four affiliates scheduled one-on-one meetings with each of the supervisors to encourage them of the value and need of this project. We were now negotiating with the Los Angeles County Board of Supervisors for $3 million. We estimated that this would be our greatest challenge to procure this amount from the supervisors. A minimum of three "yes" votes were necessary for passage of this issue.

It took a year of negotiation to secure funding from the County of Los Angeles, the City of Los Angeles, and the federal government. The combined funding provided for these four community organizations for a five-year period, amounting to $8 million. The next four months were spent organizing and hiring personnel for the four areas of the city and the County of Los Angeles which would be covered by this program.

Four area directors were hired and assigned to one of the designated areas of Los Angeles. I was assigned as area director for the Central area of Los Angeles. My job description required that I supervise 36 case workers and perform other necessary administrative duties. Phillips Temple CME Church, located in the central area of the city, was also a member of the South Central Organizing Committee. It was convenient to locate the regional office of Hope in Youth in the Phillips Temple Church. The church was more than generous with the space they provided for my office. Therefore, I reciprocated by showing my appreciation by providing them with a most generous financial remuneration each month for the space provided.

Thirty-six organizers were assigned to the South Central area of Los Angeles. They were then organized into 12 teams, each consisting of three organizers: 1. Parent Organizer, 2. Youth Organizer, 3. Parent School Organizer. The area was then divided into 12 subdivisions. A team was then assigned to each subdivision.

The youth organizers taught the youth leadership development and how to give back by doing community service. The parent/school organizer interceded between parents and school officials involving minor discipline problems. The organizer also encouraged other parents to become volunteer tutors at the school. The parent organizer brought in specialists to teach positive parenting techniques and principles. The youth organizer taught youth to engage themselves in useful community services such as graffiti removal. All of these activities were designed to empower individuals and groups to help themselves.

Prayer Ministry

The Southern California Region Annual Conference convened during the third week of August at Phillips Temple CME Church. The presiding bishop assigned me as assistant pastor of Phillips Temple (assistant pastors were assigned to selected churches during these years). During my five-year tenure at Phillips Temple, one of my responsibilities was supervising a new Hispanic congregation. This congregation initially was organized with only one family, and the worship attendance grew to 150.

This new congregation continued to grow at such an impressive rate that soon, the space became inadequate for worship. With this phenomenal growth, eventually it was necessary to move this newly organized congregation from the chapel to the fellowship hall which provided more space for worship. The Hispanic-founding pastor was ordained at the Southern Regional winter meeting. One unique aspect of his ministry was prayer. He and his wife would spend four to five hours in prayer in the nearby San Gabriel Mountains on Saturday mornings.

I might mention that I have observed that almost all growing churches have an unusually strong prayer ministry. The worship experience of the Hispanic congregation was quite different from the regular service. The service was free-flowing and several of the charismatic gifts were displayed without restraint.

EXERCISE

Jesus teaches that we must set at liberty the captives, help the blind recover their sight, and set at liberty those that are bruised. It is through social ministry that these needs are met. There are two types of social ministry: social service and social action.

a. Explain the differences between social service and social action.

_____
_____
_____
_____
_____
_____
_____

b. Give two examples of each, social service and social action.

_____
_____
_____
_____
_____
_____
_____

Chapter 7

DEVELOPING VISION

After five years of employment by an affiliate of the Industrial Areas Foundation, when the contract expired, I received a call from the pastor of a church in Dayton, Ohio, wanting to discuss a proposition with me. Pastor Washington was familiar with much of my work as he had succeeded me as pastor in Riverside, California. This pastor was also aware that I was a certified church consultant. He informed me that he was in need of a person with specific gifts and expertise. Pastor Washington asked directly what it would take for me to come to Dayton, Ohio, and accept a full-time staff position. After several weeks of negotiating, we agreed upon a rather impressive salary with all the perks. Arrangements were made for the move from California to Ohio.

On the following Saturday morning, I met with the officers of the church. This presented an opportunity for them to ask questions concerning my philosophy of ministry and for me to inquire about the position which I would be functioning in. Not only was this a new position, it was an entirely new venture. Therefore, my first assignment was to write a job description for the position.

Very early I became aware that the church had not developed a mission or vision statement. Of course, this is not a new phenomenon as so many congregations do not have a clear understanding of God's vision for ministry. Some churches do have what they call a vision statement, but it really adds up to be just a slogan. A vision statement must reflect the activities and ministry of the church.

Most Christians do not have a clear concept of what vision is. Unless the church has a clear understanding of where they are headed, the probability of obtaining their objectives is severely limited. It's more like the man who mounted his horse and rode off in all directions. Too often churches are focused on too many issues which are not related to the mandate which Jesus left with us. There is an obvious link between spiritual and numerical growth of congregations who understand God's vision for ministry. The pastor and I decided that we must begin a process of developing a mission and vision statement. The senior pastor suggested that the administrative council would meet to structure this process as there were limited materials relating to this process. We decided to create some materials ourselves.

George Barna expresses his opinion that "Most Protestant seminaries in this country virtually ignore vision as a critical dimension of ministry." It seems as if theologians, teachers, and authors do not adequately address this subject. If it is mentioned at all, it is only on a sketchy or superficial basis. Since there was limited information on how to develop vision, we had to seek this information on our own.

DEVELOPING VISION

The first and foremost approach in developing a vision statement is fasting and prayer. The next source of information concerning vision is the Bible. The Old Testament book of Nehemiah is one of the best books for studying the process of vision. The pastor's Bible Study on Sunday afternoon and Wednesday evening would teach from the book of Nehemiah.

Another method of seeking this information is by attending vision seminars conducted by reputable authorities. It is always helpful to talk to pastors who are visionary leaders. The pastor and I decided that we would pursue as many of these opportunities as possible.

PHASE I: GETTING READY FOR VISION

Prayer

Before attempting to develop a vision statement, it must begin with prayer. There is a direct relationship between vision and prayer. There are three important reasons why we must pray. The first reason is we have to be assured it is God's will. The best way we can be assured that this endeavor is God's will is through serious prayer. The second reason why we should begin with prayer is because we need God's direction to guide us through the process of developing his vision. The third reason why we must pray is because there are always "Vision Killers."

As we introduced the idea to develop a vision statement, resistance began to emerge. This resistance was the result of certain beliefs, assumptions, and even emotions. It wasn't surprising that these things came to the forefront, but we were prepared to deal with them.

Christians come to church to praise and worship God, and music plays a major role in the worship service. The pastor had stated that the type of music that the choirs were presenting does not represent his idea of the type of music which will attract greater numbers of persons to the church. The music staff were accomplished musicians, but they sensed that their rendition of music was not the preference of the pastor. The organist and director eventually resigned and accepted positions at another church.

Paul makes a statement in his letter to the Philippians, "I can do all things through Christ which strengtheneth me" (Philippians 4:13). Sometimes we are so busy doing church work that we are not able to hear God talking to us. King David was aware of this relationship between prayer and vision. "Be still and know that I am God; I will be exalted among the nations, I will be exalted in the earth" (Psalm 46:10). We must remember that when we talk to God we must also listen to God.

Several years ago, Nate, a brother-in-law who was a born-again Christian, told Tyrone, the other brother-in-law, that he talks to God. Tyrone, who was not a Christian at this time, approached me with this question. "Chester, do you talk to God?" I answered, "Yes, I talk to God, and he also talks to me." I will never forget the confused look on Tyrone's face after hearing my answer. Real communication is like a two-way street. It entails both talking and hearing. Tyrone is now a deacon in church and singing in the choir. I have no doubts now that Tyrone has conversations with God.

As there was a limited prayer ministry existing in the church, the pastor developed an effective prayer booklet to assist members in focusing their prayers on different issues and needs. We felt that prayers must be directly involved in developing a vision statement for the church. Our first approach in developing a vision statement was establishing a more effective prayer ministry. A congregational prayer meeting was organized which met on Friday evenings, 7 P.M. until 10 P.M. The participation for this event was excellent. The agenda included sharing the scriptures, testimonies, as well as oral and silent prayers. Prayers were focused on individual and congregational needs and other concerns.

Another popular event was the 6 A.M. prayer session which met daily for one hour, Monday through Friday. The church was located on a popular thoroughfare used by people on their way to work. Therefore, it was convenient for people to stop by the church to spend time in prayer before arriving at their place of employment. Several individuals were not members of the congregation but would stop by and participate in this prayer session. This prayer session was not rigidly structured. It really operated as the Holy Spirit directed. At least one of the staff pastors would attend these prayer sessions, although they didn't assume any pastoral authority. The pastors functioned merely as a resource.

Another opportunity to engage in group prayer was on Saturday mornings from 8 A.M. to 10 P.M. This was originally a men's prayer session, but over a period of time, many women began to join this group. It eventually became a mixed prayer group. After the two-hour sessions of prayer, the men would usually visit the sick that were homebound. This prayer ministry operated on the same format as the other prayer ministries.

Members were encouraged to share their testimonies during worship services. They would share how God had answered some of their prayers in a three or four-minute testimony. The time taken for these testimonies during the service did not have any negative effect on the worship experience. In fact, these testimonies were effective in reinforcing people's faith that God does answer prayer. Even as we pray, we must realize that we cannot order God to answer our prayers when we feel that they should be answered. If you feel guilty when your patience is subsiding, well, you're in good company. Think of Job in the Old Testament when he said, "All the days of my appointed time will I wait, till my change come" (Job 14:14).

Dan Sutherland makes this statement, "Vision is usually given to those who patiently wait for it." In our communities today, it seems as if we want things to happen right now. Even pastors are caught up in this expectation that things should happen instantly. It is amazing that Phillips Temple has undergone an unusual amount of transition in a relatively short time. It was necessary that we devoted an unusual amount of time in different types of prayer events to prepare for developing vision.

The challenge before us at this time was to develop a vision and mission statement for the church. The entire congregation was now ready to enter into a week of fasting and prayer. Each member received a prayer booklet which had been prepared to help focus them on fasting and praying. In this booklet were scriptures and other information which were included to help each person during the week of concerted prayer.

The administrative council met during the month for the purpose of developing a vision statement. The council proceeded with the task, knowing that many church members are sometimes referred to as vision killers. Vision killers are members who always find reasons why something can't be done. They state these seven last words when they are confronted with something new: "We never did it that way before."

One thing is certain. Pastors will always be confronted with opposition when they attempt to bring about change in a church. This type of opposition usually comes from traditional members because they are usually focused more on tradition. Many leaders are just plain tired because they are overworked, but at the same time, they are reluctant to give up these power positions. Seldom are new members resistant to new ideas or change. They are more receptive to new ideas because they are not yet bound by the traditions of the church. Having said this, I must add that many of the traditions in our churches must be preserved.

PHASE 2: PLANNING FOR VISION

There are many churches in America's communities. The question is, what differentiates one from another? They all have a form of worship, many have evangelistic outreaches, discipleship training, they help those in need, and preach the Word. It does not appear that there is much difference in what churches are doing, or attempting to do.

Among these churches there are some which do stand out. These churches have carved out a place for themselves in the community because they have found a niche. Most likely they have developed a ministry which is different from other churches in the community. Rick Warren, in his book, *The Purpose Driven Church*, teaches that every church should have a purpose and vision statement.

Some years ago when I was employed by the Los Angeles City School System as a math coordinator, after the students had finished their assignments, teachers would give them some type of fun exercises which were not directly related to the subject at hand. Sometimes this was called "busywork." Well, today, churches are just doing busywork when they aren't driven by a clear understanding of their purpose. Purpose is the driving force of vision. In reality, the purpose statement is stated clearly in the Gospel of Matthew, 28:19–20: "Go ye therefore, and teach all nations, baptizing them in the name of the Father, and of the Son, and of the Holy Ghost: Teaching them to observe all things whatsoever I have commanded you: and lo, I am with you always, even unto the end of the world."

Who Are We Trying to Reach?

Years ago when I decided to go into business manufacturing boats, I had to decide what type of boat I would build. I had to consider what type of boat a potential customer would be shopping for. Would it be for cruising, racing, fishing, or would it be necessary to have overnight accommodations? All of these desired uses would not be found in one type of boat. I eventually decided to build an 18-foot utility-type boat which could be used for several types of recreational boating. Research indicated there would be more demand for this size boat. By this approach, I was actually targeting a certain potential customer base.

Targeting is one the most controversial and misunderstood words among churches. The real question is simply, "Who are we trying to reach?" We understand that trying to reach any and everybody is not effective targeting. This is more like the shotgun approach, when the shooter aims in the general direction of his target and prays that some of the buckshot will hit something.

We learned from an analysis of our membership that most of the members were over 50. So we decided that we would design ministries which would meet the needs of people between the ages of 25 through 50. This would be our primary target. We concluded that those within this age group would have young children into the teenage years.

The secondary target would be the children and youth. Even though there is an overabundance of churches in our community, growth is possible. Why? Because research shows that 70 percent of people living in any community are either unsaved are unchurched. Jesus said unto his disciples, "The harvest truly is plenteous, but the laborers are few. Pray ye that for the Lord of the harvest, that he will send forth the laborers into his harvest" (Matthew 9:37–38).

During the years of my travels across the country conducting seminars for various churches and denominations, I have heard many pastors describe their communities by saying, "This is a Baptist community, or Methodist community, or Church of God in Christ community." I never subscribed to this analysis because I see individuals from the standpoint of are they saved or unsaved, churched or unchurched? It is interesting to note that George Barna states that on any given weekend, only about 37 percent of Americans are in church.

We have now defined our target in terms of age grouping. We now must define a target in terms of geography. Our decision is to cover a radius of 25 miles as there are several suburbs within this radius. There are three universities, and one strategic military facility, Wright-Patterson Air Force Base, within this geographical area. The demographics of this area were very near ideal as all age groups were represented and good employment opportunities abounded. These factors made it easy to reach our target.

PHASE 3: PLANTING THE VISION

We feel that we have been successful in preparing and explaining the process of vision. The success of the previous two phases of the process will assure the successful buy-in by key leaders of the church. As this is a new venture for this congregation, the leaders may feel threatened or are reluctant to give their total support to the project. We have previously organized an administrative council composed of key leaders of the church, and two at-large members. This group has also been designated to help develop the vision statement.

Our first task was to make sure our leaders and people with influence were in agreement with this project which we had undertaken. We understood that all churches have two types of leaders, official and unofficial. Sometimes unofficial leaders exert more influence in the congregation than official leaders. This type of leader is sometimes referred to as a "power broker." Power brokers are needed on any committee that is involved in change. We took the necessary time in choosing members who had the right temperament and gifts to participate on the vision committee. It has taken us a considerable amount of time in discovering our purpose and defining our vision. We are confident that this time was well spent.

Since we spent time developing our purpose and determining our target, it is essential that we develop strategies that will guide us in accomplishing our goals. We also understand that changes will have to be made. All traditional churches must change in many ways if they are to grow. That does not mean that everything has to change, but we would have to be willing to change those things that are critical to our purpose and vision.

Music is one of the first and most important things that have to change. It is also one of the most difficult things to change in our churches. But not only does it have to change, it also has to change with excellence. In fact, everything that we do in the church must be done with excellence. Each time that I was assigned to a church, I knew very early many things would have to change in order for growth to take place.

The Vision Team

We have a very effective administrative council, which is composed of individuals who have certain gifts and who are visionaries and dreamers in their thinking. It was a unanimous agreement that this council would act as the vision team. This council has worked together for a period of time and has blended together very well. The members of this group are very optimistic and feel that the sky is the limit.

Members of this group should be trustworthy and loyal. It is important that the members of this group not divulge certain discussions that take place in the committee. Certain information will be brought to the membership on a scheduled basis, usually at the church conference. This procedure is vital to the success of planting the vision. Even though much of the committee work is done behind the scenes, it is not to be secretive; the point is to be strategic.

Sometimes this is painful, but we must be bold enough to look at ourselves objectively. This could be uncomfortable, because an objective assessment of what is not working must be made. We pastors should have the courage to share our ideas and concerns with team members. Fortunately, a very close bonding exists between the members of our committee because they have been working together for a period of time. This makes it possible to deal with sensitive issues.

The senior pastor believes strongly that key leaders should be exposed to model churches. In fact, I have used this strategy many times when I was senior pastor. There are certain advantages in exposing your leadership to churches that are growing. Sometimes before initiating a new ministry, it is wise to send some of your leaders to a church that is involved in this type of ministry. Each time that I made contacts to visit progressive churches, the pastors and other officials were always very open and excited about our visit. Our leaders were able to see how the different ministries were managed. After the leaders see ministries in action, they become the most enthusiastic supporters of new ideas when brought before the church body. Eventually when a new approach of solving problems or a new idea for ministry was discussed, it was usually through those persons who had been exposed to these ideas through visiting and had observed new ways of doing things.

Those who had visited other churches were the greatest supporters of this new idea.

There is a popular axiom that says a picture is worth a thousand words. I will take the liberty of changing that to say, a practical model is worth a thousand words. I would strongly suggest to pastors that they should not be reluctant to send some of their leadership to observe other churches. This way, we don't have to reinvent the wheel; instead, all we have to do is modify the wheel to fit our specifications. Remember, life presents us with two ways of learning: we learn from personal experience, and we learn from the experience of others. Successful leaders have learned to use both of these ways of learning.

PHASE 4: PUTTING IT INTO PRACTICE

Up to this point, we have been working with a limited number of leaders who have guided us through three phases of the process. Only a few leaders in the church are aware of the vision process, namely, the vision team and power brokers. This was according to the planned strategy. It is now time to share the vision with the rest of the leaders of the church.

One thing that can run a ship onto the rocks is a lack of communication between the captain and his officers on the vessel. One strategy that I have consistently used is sharing an idea with a smaller group first. As they buy in and gain ownership, their influence and position makes it easier to sell the idea throughout the congregation. The question before the committee at this time is: how we can effectively communicate the vision to the larger group of leaders and congregation as a whole?

The Vision Retreat

For the past five weeks, we have concentrated our efforts on getting ready for vision, planning for vision, and planting the vision. Only a small group of members have participated in the vision process. Even though there was an understanding that this group was asked not to discuss this project with anyone at this point, it was no surprise that this information had leaked out, and, as usual, all of the information received was not altogether correct.

The last thing that we would want to happen was for leaders feeling that they were being left out of the planning. There was a possibility that some collateral damage could develop. All persons involved in the vision committee agreed that we should share the vision with a larger group of leaders. The best venue for this would be to plan a six-hour retreat away from our facility.

Reservations were made at a retreat center in a nearby community. A date was set, and the necessary information went to all leaders of the congregation. This being such an important event, it was announced in both church services. Each leader received a written invitation to attend, and even a telephone tree was organized. By using this strategy, more than 90 percent of the leaders were present at the retreat.

Two important items on the agenda were presented at the retreat: (1) presenting the vision to the leaders present at the retreat, (2) planning how to present and explain the vision statement to the entire membership.

After the routine of opening with prayer and scriptures from the Bible, I, as senior pastor, commented regarding the purpose of the meeting. I also stated what I would like to see accomplished.

The meeting coordinator then called the vision committee to make their report. She stated that they had put in quite a bit of time and effort in developing a vision statement. She asked for individuals to remove the vision statement from their folder but to not attempt to read it at this time as it would be projected on the screen through PowerPoint.

The Vision Statement

We desire to be a people empowered by the Holy Spirit to:
- Worship God
- Work with one another
- Witness to the world
- Welcome all people

You will note that the statement covers four major areas of ministry which clearly represents our mission at Phillips Temple. The annual budget reflects the needs of these four areas of ministry. After presenting this vision statement to the leaders, some questions were asked and answered. Then the statement was accepted in its original form.

The issue before us is how we will share this vision with the remainder of the church. The last session of the retreat provided opportunities for every person to participate by offering ideas how to share the vision with the entire membership. Members were urged to give their ideas regardless of how absurd it might seem. As the ideas were offered, they were projected on the screen. Here are some samples of these ideas:

- The senior pastor and staff pastors would preach a series of sermons on vision from the books of Nehemiah and Acts. One of the assets that the senior pastor possesses is biblical preaching. In fact, I feel strongly that every sermon preached should have something to do with vision.
- The vision statement is displayed on a large banner on the wall behind the pulpit and choir stand. The congregation repeats the vision statement at the beginning of each worship service. Reading the statement regularly serves to impress it in each person's memory.
- Whenever the staff attended vision conferences or church growth conferences, tapes, CDs, and other materials were usually brought back for those who were not able to attend.

EXERCISE

1. Before attempting to develop vision, it must begin with _____.

There are three reasons why we must begin with prayer.
Circle the best answer
   a. To be a sure that it is God's will
   b. To ask God for his direction
   c. Because of vision killers
   d. All of the above

2. Describe three ways how you could share the vision with the congregation.

_____
_____
_____
_____
_____
_____
_____

Chapter 8

LEADERSHIP—MAKING IT HAPPEN

A considerable amount of time has been spent trying to choose a title for this chapter. Originally I had decided to focus on the word "administration," but as I gave more thought to this, I changed. "Leadership" is a more inclusive term than the word "administration." An administrator's effectiveness depends upon his/her leadership ability. Leadership is different from managing, teaching, counseling, and helping. We usually expect the pastor to have leadership ability, but too often they are acting more as managers or administrators. These other gifts and talents are valuable, but they must not be substituted for leadership. Leadership focuses on relationships, and this has to do with how effective a relationship is managed.

There is a difference between leaders and managers, and we can distinguish these differences by how they relate to people and also by their focus on goal objectives. Leaders must be innovative and have an unusual ability to involve people in reaching their goals.

The concept of leadership implies change and movement. A leader moves his followers from where they are to where they should be. This process suggests change in direction, change in ideas, and sometimes a change in location.

Pastors are usually confronted with resistance when they try to implement change. Pastors must be bold enough to assume the position of innovator to bring about change, although when they offer an innovative idea they are usually confronted by resistance. I experienced a classic example of resistance when I decided to start an eight o'clock service in my second charge. Surprisingly, resistance to this idea came full circle from all areas of the church, even though the proposal was presented in such a way that it was obvious that another service would enhance growth. The proposal was passed in the church conference by a reasonable majority, but it seemed as if something else was taking place outside of the official meeting. This turned out to be a learning experience in realizing that a majority vote doesn't always reflect how members really feel about an issue.

I was even accused of dividing the church by initiating an eight o'clock service. At this point, I was strongly committed to the idea that another service was necessary since the sanctuary was more than 80 percent full at the 11 o'clock worship service.

In spite of strong resistance, I made this decision because research supports this principle of growth. This was another way of increasing the capacity of the sanctuary. In a very short time, the eight o'clock service was rivaling the 11 o'clock worship service, and the congregation was very happy with this outcome.

The Bible shows that leadership happens when it occurs in the context of a gifted team of people in support of a leader who has been called and gifted by God for the purpose of leading. Moses had Joshua and Aaron; Jesus had Peter, James, and John; and Paul had Timothy, Luke, and Titus. Paul writes in I Corinthians 12:7, every believer is given a gift to be used "For the common good" (KJV). Unfortunately, members sometimes have a tendency to place certain gifts in a position above others. No gift is any more important than any other. Pastors need all the gifts active in the congregation to be successful as a pastor. Although sometimes it is a challenge to accomplish this goal, the pastors must make every effort to know the spiritual gifts that God has placed in their congregation.

Early in my first pastorate, I believe it was a stroke of luck when Gail and Robert Moore united with Emmanuel Temple Church. Sgt. Moore was an airman stationed at George Air Force Base, located just two miles from my church. He was licensed to preach by another major denomination, the Church Of God In Christ. In addition to his gift of preaching, I became aware that this young man had other gifts, such as leadership and administration. This was borne out as he took the initiative in developing certain projects in the church. In addition to these gifts, he would consistently take the initiative to create new ministries.

I am of the opinion that too often pastors are reluctant to take the initiative in bringing about change. There is an unofficial rule that states that it is easier to ask for forgiveness than to ask for permission. Rev. Moore was a godsend because I had to travel almost 200 miles round-trip to my church. During this period, I was employed by the Los Angeles City School System and made this trip two to three times each week. This young man was very creative and took the initiative in doing ministry. Needless to say, Rev. Moore was an important addition to my staff. He served with us for a period of 2½ years and much was accomplished during this period.

From this experience, I learned how to delegate responsibility and this principle of leadership became a mainstay of my ministry. I found that when additional staff was added, whether volunteer or paid, churches experienced growth.

Usually the first consideration in adding staff is the cost. Yes, it will cost because training and materials are necessary for any significant ministry. Of course, a congregation must be of a certain size to be able to hire paid staff. There are two other options to consider: (1) to develop a strong volunteer ministry, and this is the option most churches with an attendance below 200 choose to do. There are limitations when depending on volunteers to chair certain ministries, however. When people volunteer their service, they are not really obligated to be there at certain designated hours. (2) Arrange to pay a stipend to a part-time worker. The worker functioning under this condition feels that the job he is doing is important. When workers are paid to render a certain service, they are obligated to be there to fulfill the contract. In other words, when something urgent occurs, the volunteer worker will likely see this as a higher priority than his volunteer work, so he will usually take care of this issue first. On the other hand, if the worker is on salary or stipend, they will feel even more obligated to fulfill his contractual agreement with the church. These conditions hold true whether it is an oral or written contract.

One of the problems with oral agreements is over a period of time parties forget the details of these agreements. I have made it a practice to have written job descriptions for every ministry head. This process helps to create positive relationships with those who volunteer to head certain ministries in the church. The pastor as a Christian leader is also required to be a good manager (administrator).

Leadership focuses on relationships, and this has to do with how effective relationships are managed. There is a difference between leaders and managers, and we can distinguish these differences by how they relate to people and also by their focus on goal objectives. Leaders must be innovative and have an unusual ability to involve people in reaching their goals and take advantage of opportunities to further develop their skills.

There are several ways to keep abreast of new trends and new ways of doing things. We live in a world where changes are taking place at such a rapid rate that we are not aware of the impact on our ministries. Our programs of ministry may not be meeting the needs of people today.

We must understand that there are no patents on leadership principles and methods. Some pastors may be reluctant to send their members to another church to observe how they are doing things for fear that they may consider joining that church. Pastors who are confident in themselves and their ministries would not hesitate to send members to visit other churches to observe how other churches are doing ministry.

There are many opportunities available for learning more about leadership. It may be expedient for pastors to take advantage by attending seminars and conferences on leadership and a variety of other subjects sponsored by mega-churches or para-church organizations. Conferences and seminars of this type are more effective simply because more time is available to teach one discipline. Many seminars of this type are available in all areas of the country.

Leadership Training

Several years ago, I was engaged in a conversation with a denominational official and the topic centered on leadership. This official stated that they didn't have enough pastors with leadership qualities. I was very surprised to hear him make such a statement. My response to this statement was, if they don't have these qualities of leadership, why not just teach them leadership principles and methods? My response was based on the fact that I had been a master teacher in the Los Angeles City School System. For a period of seven years, I trained prospective teachers from the University of Southern California. It was only natural that I would respond in this manner because I am convinced that everyone can learn. As I gave some thought to this statement, I concluded that there could be some truth in it because there are differences in people's learning curve.

One morning, the senior pastor called my office and asked me to come down to his office as he wanted to speak with me. He related to me that he would like to carry our leaders of the different ministries to Southeastern Christian Church in Louisville, Kentucky. Pastor Washington asked that I call this church and make arrangements for a visit bringing our chairpersons of ministries with us. After concluding the conference with the senior pastor, I put in a call to Southeastern Community Church to see if they would be amenable to this request. I must admit that I was somewhat uncomfortable in making this contact and asking such a request. To my surprise, the leaders of this church were really excited about the opportunity to help another church. They immediately checked the calendar and gave us an option of three different dates. The administrator suggested the Wednesday date as most of their leaders would be at the church on Wednesdays because they have a midweek worship service. When reporting to the senior pastor regarding the results of this contact, he was very pleased with these arrangements.

Upon arriving at this church, we were awed by the magnitude of this structure. It is said that this church has the largest physical structure of any church in the country. As we entered the parking lot, we were directed to a special area to park our vehicles. These greeters accompanied us to a large conference room, where we were greeted by the senior pastor who gave us a warm welcome. He then introduced Carol, the person who would be in charge of coordinating our visit. She explained that the first item on our agenda would be a complete tour of the facility.

As we toured the facility, Carol explained how the different areas of this facility were utilized. She was very patient answering the many questions which were asked. This tour took about 40 minutes. We assembled again in the conference room, where we were introduced to each chairperson of the various ministries at Southeastern. These chairpersons gave a brief explanation of how they manage their ministries.

LEADERSHIP—MAKING IT HAPPEN

After a brief question-and-answer period, the chairmen of our ministries (youth workers, children's workers, adult workers, evangelism, and Christian education) were paired with similar chairmen of the Southeastern Church. These pairs spent considerable time together to experience firsthand how these ministries operated.

Southeastern has a worship service on Wednesday evening, and they insisted that we stay and experience this event. After experiencing this dynamic worship service we were happy that we stayed as we were richly blessed. We then returned to Dayton, Ohio.

At our next staff meeting, we evaluated the experience of visiting Southeastern Christian Church in Louisville, Kentucky. The first thing which stood out was the friendliness of this congregation. We were met as we entered the parking lot by greeters, who ushered us to the entrance of the building. Not only were they friendly, but they seem to really enjoy making us comfortable in every way. Everyone that we came in contact with greeted us with a smile. One of the church growth principles is friendliness. A friendly congregation is a growing congregation.

We also learned that workers who desire to work in ministries must undergo training. This could be compared to some type of apprenticeship. In addition to this training, some were then designated to be trained in leadership principles and methods. This training provides a database of trained persons able to assume leadership positions whenever the need arises.

The INJOY Leadership Training Opportunity

The INJOY Group was founded by John Maxwell in 1985. Its primary purpose is helping churches reach their potential by teaching leadership skills through seminars and conferences. INJOY extended a personal invitation to the pastor and leaders of Phillips Temple to come to their headquarters in Atlanta, Georgia, for a personal seminar on leadership. We were not surprised to receive this invitation because this same group had directed a successful financial campaign for our church. The title of the seminar to be presented was: "The Twenty-One Irrefutable Laws of Leadership." This seminar is one of John Maxwell's most popular seminars, which is presented in different areas of the country yearly.

In this presentation, we learned about the 21 leadership laws. They are not based on culture, gender, or even age. These laws are workable in all communities. We focused on several of these laws which were relevant to our particular situation. I feel strongly that there is a need to raise up a new generation of leaders in our churches who can identify and understand the pressing issues in our society today. We must understand that real ministry happens at the local church, and it has to respond to the issues in its local community. Even though many of the issues are similar, yet there are unique problems to be addressed in different communities. Leaders must have a sense of intuition, which makes it possible for them to read people and the environment in which we live. Pastors with this sense of intuition are able to take advantage of opportunities which arise in their communities. In other words, there are always opportunities to be addressed in every community.

A leader's effectiveness depends upon those who are closest to him. This circle of friends and advisers is what is referred to as the "inner circle." When leaders choose people who will make up the inner circle, they must choose those who have more expertise in certain areas than they do. I'm sure that many might disagree with this statement; therefore, I will explain why I am committed to this idea. The leader must surround himself with those who have expertise and knowledge in areas where he may be lacking. This knowledge is needed to implement his vision. If the members of the inner circle do not bring to the table the necessary expertise and knowledge, then they have very little to offer concerning the growth and development of the church.

The pastor of Phillips Temple Church began putting together an inner circle by adding me as a consultant and full-time staff pastor. I will share how this process developed. I was nearing the end of a five-year contract with a nonprofit affiliate of the Industrial Areas Foundation. One afternoon, I received a phone call from James Washington, the pastor of Phillips Temple Church in Dayton, Ohio. I was familiar with the pastor as he succeeded the pastor at Amos Temple Church in Riverside, California. Temple is a well organized 400-member congregation and blessed with an abundance of administrative talent.

Pastor Washington came right to the point as he stated that he needed my expertise as a full-time staff pastor. I really wasn't enthused with this idea as I had spent six years as a pastor in northern California. Pastor Washington must have suspected that I wasn't too enthusiastic about his proposal because he immediately asked what it would take for me to come to Dayton. I began to realize that Pastor Washington was in command of this conversation. After gaining my composure, I suggested that I would like to think this over for at least a couple of days. He readily agreed to this suggestion.

Exactly two days later, Pastor Washington called again, as he had promised, and asked if I had made a decision. He also stated that he had been following my ministry and was impressed with how churches had grown under my administration. He was aware that I have a certification as a church growth consultant. He again asked what it would take for me to join his staff.

It began to dawn on me at this point that this pastor was very serious about his proposition. I informed him that in addition to my salary, I would need a parsonage and all expenses in maintaining it. His immediate response was, "You got it." The next item that I presented to him was that the church must pay my retirement, which he agreed to. Since I was now on a roll, I decided to push it all the way. I asked that a certain amount would be put in my budget for seminars and conferences for my professional growth, which would include transportation, lodging, and per diem for meals. The pastor informed me that these items are provided through another budget. Pastor Washington and I eventually agreed to this generous package. Therefore, I graciously accepted the position of director of Discipleship Ministries.

During the next month, two telephone conferences were arranged so that key officers of Phillips Temple could ask questions concerning my education, marriage status, pastoral history, and other questions relevant to this new position. I later learned that they had completed a process of vetting and apparently they were satisfied with the results. The trustee chairman suggested that someone should be provided to assist me in driving from California to Dayton. The church provided the funds for the driver and his airfare back to California. The trip took three-and-a-half days and we arrived on the third day at approximately three P.M.

We were met at the church by the trustees who informed us that our baggage which was shipped had not arrived but that they would be delivered the next day. In the meantime, we were taken to the three-bedroom house which had been leased for my residence. The pastor arrived at this residence at about the same time. While our belongings were being unloaded and placed inside the house, the pastor suggested that we go to a restaurant for dinner. After dinner we returned to our residence as we were ready to retire for the evening.

After breakfast the next morning, the pastor picked us up and we returned to the church. He then introduced me to the office staff and gave me a tour of the facility. The facility was well kept. He showed me two vacant offices on the second floor of the education unit which were adjacent to each other. He stated that I could choose either of the two.

The following week, my office was furnished with new furniture and a computer. The next week was spent in meeting with ministry chairpersons. This was the beginning of an exciting and significant nine-year adventure in church growth.

Soon after I had settled into my new position at Phillips Temple Church in Dayton, Ohio, the pastor confided in me that he felt that if this church was going to experience growth, the music would have to change to be more appealing to a greater population. He stated that this would be the highest priority at this time. Realizing that music is a very sensitive issue in churches, the pastor was searching for some way to deal with this issue. Pastor Washington suggested that we would give some thought on how to approach this issue. We also decided that we would go into concerted prayer, asking God to guide us in making the right decisions concerning the music department.

We set aside an hour each day for a period of two weeks to pray for God's guidance concerning the music department. The choir director and organist were accomplished musicians and had been a great asset to the music department through the years. The choir was well trained and their rendition of hymns and anthems was superb. At this time the worship was strictly liturgical, sometimes referred to as "high church." Even the seating of the choir was of such that there were two sections facing each other instead of facing the audience. With all of this being true, they could not produce the type of music which the pastor thought would attract new members.

In the meantime, the pastor and I decided to make some strategic changes in the layout of the choir stand. Contractors were brought in and changed the whole configuration of the choir section. The congregation was very happy about the changes that were made, but the musicians felt that this was the straw that broke the camel's back. All of the musicians gracefully turned in their resignations without any obvious hostility or animosity. The changes in the music department became more contemporary. This was an excellent decision as our new choir became well-known in the community and was asked to furnish music at many events in the community such as the county fair. The choir contributed to the phenomenal growth of Phillips Temple Church over a period of time.

Two factors were involved in the smooth transition of the music department. (1) The power of prayer and (2) The right timing. One of the laws of leadership is timing, which is doing the right thing at the right time. We exercised patience before we initiated the idea of making changes in the music department. The Psalmist writes, "These that wait upon thee; thou may give them their meat in due season" (Psalm 37:7).

I believe that some leaders have a sense of intuition which makes it possible for them to seize opportunities when they arise. There was a well organized ministry of children ages five through twelve meeting on Saturday mornings at the Boys and Girls Club across the street from our church. Eventually, there was a problem of available space, and the club could no longer provide space for their activities.

Dave, a businessman, was providing financial support and supervision for this group. Jason was a very creative teacher in the Dayton Unified School System. Dave and Jason were the primary people who were maintaining this ministry. Phillips Temple was directly across the street from the Boys and Girls Club, and the director contacted us and asked if we could provide space for this Saturday morning program. My focus in ministry has always been social ministries, which involves reaching out into the community. This was an opportunity to reach out and establish relationships with a greater number of people who were unchurched or unsaved. Therefore, my response was to offer them what I considered a more meaningful proposition. Not only would we offer them space for the ministry, we would consider making this ministry a part of the ministries of Phillips Temple. Dave and Jason were surprised at this suggestion and readily agreed to this opportunity. The pastor was also enthused with this idea and proceeded to clear this through the proper channels. I continued to add staff to this new ministry.

We proceeded to reorganize the His Kids Ministry in such a way that it would service a greater number of children. We formed a joint venture with a suburban congregation and eventually were able to operate on a budget of $50,000 yearly. Part of the budget was allotted for transportation. Each church provided a 50-passenger bus for picking up the children on Saturday morning.

Our staff was composed of about 30 committed volunteers who had been trained for this ministry. As usual, unanticipated problems arose as we transitioned this ministry into Phillips Temple. Some of the members weren't very happy to see 150 children from public housing in the church each Saturday morning. I witnessed one incident where an elderly lady had Dave cornered in the hall and, shaking her finger in his face, said, "These children are tearing up our church." It was fortunate that I was nearby and was able to put out this fire.

How was the name "His Kids" given to this ministry? When we first adopted this ministry, Dave was recognized as the person in charge of it and literally saw the kids as belonging to him. It was apparent that the members had not yet accepted this group of children as a part of the church ministry. We were eventually successful in convincing the congregation that they were an official ministry of the church. The name His Kids stuck, but it was interpreted that they were God's children, not Dave's.

Worship Service for the Homeless

Our food program provided hot balanced meals for the homeless each Wednesday. We announced to people attending this ministry that we were starting a brief worship service before serving lunch. We couldn't require anyone to attend the worship service although some thought it was mandatory. It just happened that our memory didn't serve us very well, and we would usually forget to mention that it was not mandatory to attend. An average of 40 people would attend the brief worship service. As time passed, many of them began to ask if they could read the scripture, pray, or give a testimony. They had actually bought in to this service and recognized that it was their own. Interestingly, none of them united with the church as they would likely feel uncomfortable worshipping in a traditional church service.

Often, people in the general population see the homeless as being shiftless and irresponsible, but I have learned that this is not always true. Over the years, I have come to another conclusion. Many of the homeless are victims of situations that caused them to be homeless such as loss of employment or lack of transportation. Many of these people do not have a support system to help them better themselves. I have always made a point in my ministry to take advantage of opportunities, and there are *always* opportunities in every situation. We must always seek out these opportunities. Sometimes help comes from sources near us.

Barbara was a new member who had taken an interest in our feeding ministry. She seemed to have had a special interest in the problems of the homeless. She arranged a conference with me to discuss a proposal. At the conference, she presented a plan to help homeless people find employment. Barbara stated that the homeless usually didn't have funds to use the public transportation to look for jobs. We decided that a proposal should be written and submitted to the Municipal Transportation System, asking for tokens for homeless people who were looking for employment. We were pleasantly surprised when we received an answer to our request in a week and a half. The public relations official informed us that they would furnish as many as 1,000 tokens each year for this purpose. Realizing that sometimes there are abuses in programs of this type, safeguards were built in to protect the integrity of the ministry. We also submitted monthly reports to the agency supplying the tokens.

EXERCISE

When in positions of leadership, difficult decisions have to be made. Resistance to the issue may be prevalent. Which of the following is the best under a difficult situation?

a. Insist on your approach to the problem.
b. Let the other parties make the decision.
c. Offer an alternative which would be a compromise.

CHAPTER 9

WORSHIP

Principle #8: Churches grow when worship is done with excellence

Dynamic corporate worship is the basic building block of church growth. Churches grow when there is dynamic corporate worship. The Sunday morning worship hour is the time when the congregation comes together to celebrate. This celebration is also an entry point to the church. This is the time the visitor will make a decision whether to unite with the church or perhaps return as a visitor at another time.

In many churches, the preliminaries are considered just a warm-up before the main event, which is the sermon. It seems as if we look upon the sermon as more important than the participation of the congregation in adoration, praise, confession, thanksgiving, and dedication. All of these aforementioned items are equally important in real worship. As long as this erroneous attitude prevails, the worship will not be done well. Rather than attracting people to Christ, we are, in essence, sending them away because seldom do visitors return for a second visit. It is obvious that we must rethink our attitude towards worship.

What do you feel or think about when you hear the word "worship"? It is likely that several things come to mind, such as singing, praying, preaching, or even announcements. It is important that the worshiper enter the sanctuary with the right attitude toward worship. Worship requires preparation of the heart. It involves waiting. It requires refocusing the mind and heart from self, others, and life to God.

As we enter God's sanctuary on Sunday morning, often we are physically quiet but our minds are still racing and occupied with what went on before the service. We adjust to the quiet atmosphere, but we seldom focus on God. We usually fix our attention on the details of the service. We read with interest or disinterest news in the bulletin. We note that the choir is either "on" or "off" today. We look around to see who is there. We fight going to sleep; we stand up and sit down several times. We may fill out an assortment of cards, then settle down to listen to the sermon. We then wait eagerly for the words, "Let us all stand for the benediction," which signals the end of the worship.

What has taken place? We have been sung to, preached at, told about coming events, but have not really worshipped. Could it be that God did not receive anything from us? We were in too big a hurry; we were not prepared. To worship is to be in touch with God—to pray to God, to sing to God, to confess to God, and to respond to God as he is revealed in his Word. Our purpose should be to give something, not to receive something. Oh yes, we will be blessed, but these blessings will be a result of our giving.

Christians throughout the land leave worship every Sunday feeling cheated. This would hardly be true if they were singing, praying, and responding joyfully, enthusiastically, and full of vitality. Lively worship services have a very definite influence on the numerical growth of the church. A church which has a genuine enthusiastic worship will draw people.

The worship service is the entry point for the great majority of members. Visitors usually come to the worship service first. If the first experience is positive, meaningful, and uplifting, the visitor will return and most likely get involved in other areas of the church activities. Adequate financial support must be provided to make the worship service an attractive part of the life of the church. The worship service, more than anything else, determines the climate, or atmosphere, of the church.

Corporate worship provides an opportunity for unity in the body of Christ. Members function in different interest groups, but the corporate worship service provides the occasion when all the diverse groups come together in joyful unity.

God wants our worship more than anything else. The worship experience is central to the church's purpose. A dying church will not be a worshipping church. A divided church will not be a worshipping church. When people come to worship, the experience should be a positive and meaningful one.

When in worship do you sometimes feel bored or empty on the inside? If people answer honestly, you will get a pretty good understanding of what they really think about worship. What people think and feel about worship will either have a negative or positive affect on how they respond in worship.

Today, people have formed negative attitudes about traditional worship. The music in many churches is unappealing to a large segment of the population. Announcements consume too much time; there is too much liturgy and dull sermons. To reach the postmodern culture, service must be more upbeat and music has to be contemporary. There should be minimal time making announcements. When worship is poorly, done it is usually irrelevant and boring.

Rather than attracting people to Christ, many churches are turning people away. Too often when the unchurched visitors come to worship they don't return after the first visit. Our young people generally stay with us until they enter their teens. Eventually, their parents give up because it is too much of a hassle to make them attend church. What can pastors and church planters do about this situation?

We need to take a critical look at our mode of worship if we are not attracting people to a worship service. Our traditional style of worship was effective in the church culture of the forties and fifties, but that isn't relevant in the contemporary society today. There are certain things which must be changed to ensure meaningful worship. People prefer instruments which are more popular, such as guitars, keyboards, and certainly in the black church, Hammond organs. To reach the postmodern culture, the music must be more upbeat and contemporary. You will remember that John and Charles Wesley were thoroughly contemporary in taking tunes from the pubs (taverns) in England. There should be minimal time in making announcements, and it should not last more than four minutes.

Worship Must Be Done with Excellence

The first consideration to reassure excellence in worship is to maintain discipline. Choir directors and other music personnel should be in their positions at a reasonable time before the worship service begins. Other ministries such as greeters, ushers, and parking attendants also play a significant part in making the worship experience appealing. The friendliness and concern shown by these groups is appreciated by the visitors as they serve to create a positive mood to worship.

As I just noted, John Wesley's music was contemporary in his time but that same music today is looked upon as traditional music. Could it be what is contemporary music today will be looked upon as traditional music in the future? It's interesting to note that society is always in a state of change. Our preferences of church music has also been caught in these changes.

Leaders Must Be Worshipers

Leaders must be authentic worshipers of Christ. In the past, pastors involved themselves in public worship through preaching and prayer. The trend today is toward more pastoral involvement in other areas of worship such as leading the congregation in corporate adoration, thanksgiving, commitment, and prayer. This type of leadership requires much time spent in private prayer on the part of pastoral leaders and anyone else who leads God's people in worship.

Worship Should Be Culturally Relevant

The worship bulletin should be prepared with visitors in mind because they form first impressions as they survey the events to take place in the service. It must be simple enough to meet the needs of both the visitors and members. The bulletin should be kept simple because visitors do not always understand much of the church ritual. I have observed some worship services where the announcements take as much as 12 minutes. Afterward, it takes the choir quite awhile to reestablish the worshiping spirit.

An invitation to unite with the church should be extended at every service. I emphasize this because some churches do not extend an invitation in each service. When the invitation is extended to the worshipers to unite with the church, the person announcing this explains briefly how the church accepts new members. This is an important step because there are certain requirements before being accepted as a regular member of the church. An alternative method is sometimes used by some churches, where an Information Card is inserted in the bulletin, and the visitor is asked to fill in certain personal information.

There has been a paradigm shift in our society today. In the past when persons moved from one location to another, they usually chose a new church on the basis of denominational affiliation or doctrine, not on the basis of worship style. Even though the style of worship was important, doctrine was the final criteria. The priorities were (1) doctrine, (2) name, and (3) denomination. Different denominations had a characteristic style of worship, and their members were loyal to it. Because denominations were relatively homogeneous, people could transfer from one church to another and adjust easily because there was little difference from one congregation to another. This is no longer true because of the changes which have taken place in society.

People usually chose mainline churches with such names as First Methodist Church, First Presbyterian, First A.M.E, Trinity Church, etc. People were familiar with these names and what they reflected. It is interesting to note that some of churches are named after individuals, but people are not particularly attracted to a church that is named after a person. Churches with names such as Pentecostal or Sanctified were not popular choices years ago. These churches or denominations were looked upon by mainline churches as sects, or maybe even an outcast group. These attitudes began to change during the fifties and sixties, and some of these churches are recognized today as legitimate institutions.

Styles of Worship

As we observe worship from a broad standpoint, we understand that there are two styles of worship, namely "high church" and "low church." For our purposes, we will refer to them as "liturgical worship" or "informal-style worship." Liturgical worship usually follows an order of events such as the Doxology, the Lord's Prayer, responsive reading of scripture, a choral response after the pastoral prayer, the Gloria Patri, and the singing of "Amen" at the ending of each hymn.

The second type of worship came from groups that did not come out of the mainstream of the reformation, which included groups like the Methodist, Baptist, Mennonites, and Brethren. These were usually led by pastors without education who preached extemporaneously without a manuscript. These services included testimonies, prayers, and shouts of "Amen" and "Hallelujah."

As I describe the different types of worship style, you will find there is a blending of worship practices in different churches and denominations. The liturgical and charismatic styles of worship are more easily recognized as the styles are quite obvious.

Liturgical Churches

In some churches, the style of worship has not changed since the denomination was founded. Many congregations are still singing hymns that were sung by their grandparents. This style of worship is not as viable today as it was in the past. Some of these worshipers feel that they are invigorated with this type of worship service. The members of liturgical services are not focused on evangelism, learning, and fellowshipping. They feel that it is enough to be obedient to God. Statistics show that many of these churches or denominations are declining because they are resistant to change.

Charismatic Churches

The charismatic style of worship is characterized by feeling and activity. Worshipers feel free to lift their hands and freely clap in worship. They sing praise songs and go to the altar to pray. They lay hands on one another for healing. Most of the charismatic churches emphasize the miraculous gifts of tongues, healing, and slaying in the spirit. Not all charismatic renewal churches are practicing the Pentecostal style of worship. These classifications are more like a blending of several types of worship. The Charismatic-Pentecostal worship may be found in many mainline or liturgical churches such as Methodist, Presbyterian, or even some Roman Catholic churches. Saint Brigid Catholic Church and Amos Temple Methodist Church, located in the central area of Los Angeles, are examples of a Charismatic-Pentecostal blended type of worship.

The Bible Word Church

This type of worship service shows sermon notes by PowerPoint onto a screen as people follow the sermon outline. These pastors are gifted in teaching and usually make references to the original languages of the Bible. This type of worship crosses denominational lines and is used in Baptist, Presbyterian, Methodist, and Independent Bible churches. Many of these pastors have received their education or training from a Bible college or para-church organization such as Navigators or Campus Crusade.

Evaluation

Evaluation of the worship should be done on a regular basis. Some churches have placed the responsibility of evaluating the worship service on the worship committee. An administrative council has been established by some churches for the purpose of evaluating the total ministry of the church. These groups meet weekly, and one of their priority items is evaluating the worship service. The worship committee or the administrative council should ask, "What did we do well? What must we do to improve? How did visitors respond to the worship service?"

Many events are necessary for the worship service to be effective in meeting the needs of members. A congregation must hear the preached Word and this must be relevant to their lives as they live each day. There are certain principles necessary in building and preaching the sermon.

First, if we are going to attract the unchurched people, the sermon should not be boring. A strong sermon should begin with some type of interesting story or news event. Sometimes we preachers lose it early in our opening statements. Preachers should feel free to use illustrations where necessary to bring out some specific point in their presentations.

It is a fact that people respond to sermons which address their felt needs. Pastors should make an effort to know where people hurt. Much information comes through informal conversations. Most pastors know how to encourage people to communicate the challenges in their lives.

Few people are interested in the theology of the Bible. They are more interested in a practical application of the scriptures to their lives. Yes, people are interested in the hereafter, but the great majority is more interested in what's going to happen at the end of the week. This is why I think it is important to preach "How To ..." sermons. *How to be a good parent; How to be a good husband/wife; How to succeed in school; How to choose a mate,* etc.

It is normal for preachers to use biblical terms in their sermons such as, "born-again," "repent," "saved," "redemption," and other terms which the unsaved do not understand. It is important for the preacher to use contemporary language in his presentation so that the listeners understand. The sermon is more effective if it is communicated in a positive way.

I have observed that churches are moving into media presentations in the worship service. Announcements and other information are projected onto a large screen during the worship service. This is far more efficient than a person coming forward reading a series of announcements which take valuable time from the worship. Pastors can be very creative in using media.

EXERCISE

1. Briefly describe the worship that takes place in your church today.

   _____
   _____
   _____
   _____

2. What are the strengths and weaknesses of the worship in your church?

   _____
   _____
   _____
   _____

3. What are the components necessary for real worship?

   _____
   _____
   _____
   _____

Chapter 10

CHURCH ADMINISTRATION FOR TODAY

When we use the terms "administration," "management," and "leadership," we must understand that sometimes these words are used interchangeably depending upon the context. First of all, pastors are administrators because they are ultimately responsible for the total operation of the church. For our purposes, I will explain how these words are used in this book. Even though "leadership" and "management" are sometimes used interchangeably, there are differences in their meanings.

Managers are concerned that things work as planned. The first consideration is there must be a plan. After a plan is formulated, it must be followed; otherwise, there is no use in having a plan. Managers usually organize to accomplish short-range objectives. They take care of details.

Leaders have the ability to create a vision for the future. Leaders are able to create a better future by taking advantage of opportunities. Usually they are able to envision things that may happen in the future. On one of my consultation services, I was responsible for managing 55 ministries. Each of these ministries had a person designated as the leader of that small group. Those in charge of the group would be functioning as a leader in relationship to the members of that group. Each of the group leaders were functioning as a manager in their relationship to me as the director of all of the small group ministries.

To be a successful pastor, one must accept and understand the threefold responsibility of pastoring: preaching, pastoral service, and administration. Most pastors have preached good sermons to full churches, and sometimes to empty pews. Often, pastors have become discouraged because they have not been as successful in managing the affairs of the church. The responsibilities of the pastor in today's society have undergone changes to such an extent that pastors have not always been able to meet the challenges of a changing society today. Managers must position themselves to take advantage of these changes. It is difficult for them to adjust to these changes that are taking place at such a fast rate. This is a different world, a world which is always in a state of continuous change. This is just one of the many reasons why so many of our churches and denominations have reached a plateau or experienced serious decline during the past 40 years.

It remains that the pastor is ultimately responsible for every activity, every event, and every program of ministry in the church. Years ago, President Harry S. Truman expressed it this way: "The buck stops here." Experience has shown that a pastor can only effectively serve approximately 200 to 250 members in the church. Even to accommodate these numbers the pastor must delegate some authority to volunteer leaders in the church.

This is somewhat difficult for some pastors to do because of their preferred type of administration.

In biblical times, leaders delegated much of their responsibility. Consider Nehemiah who preached while he undertook the project of rebuilding the walls of Jerusalem and Daniel who found time to rule the providences of Babylon and to preside as chief of the governors and the wise men while he prophesied and preached. Not only did Moses undertake the problem of leading the Israelite people out of Egypt, but he also spent a great amount of time teaching them the law which God had given on Mount Sinai. We can see that these leaders, managers, or administrators were also effective in multitasking when the occasion required.

Decision Making

Making decisions is one of the most crucial factors in determining the effectiveness of an administrator. This is an area where many administrators or managers are lacking in ability. It is likely that many leaders are reluctant to make difficult decisions because of the possibility of negative ramifications. Sometime leaders are too hasty in making decisions because they believe the members may view them as being indecisive or weak as a leader.

I think it would be wise to review a method I have utilized in making decisions. In makings decisions, I usually proceed through a process to be certain that I have all the necessary factual information to make a satisfactory decision. Note that I used the word "satisfactory." The context implies that it may not be popular or agreeable to all, but it does suggest that the decision was based on factual information. It is rare that a decision turns out wrong when it is based on reliable information.

The first action is to gather the facts concerning the issue at hand. After gathering pertinent information relating to the issue, I proceed to make a detailed analysis of the facts. Many times, churches are dealing with issues without gathering the necessary facts to make a well-informed decision. There have been rare occasions when wisdom dictated that it would be best to table the issue temporarily. This action eliminates the possibility of the problem developing into a chaotic situation.

Whether the congregation receives the decision negatively or positively, we learn through this process how the decision will impact the congregation. Even if the decision is rejected by the board, the issue can be brought back at a more opportune time. This provides an opportunity to rework or modify the proposal before bringing it back to the conference. One important lesson we learn through experience is that rejection is not always defeat. It is possible to learn something from every encounter, whether it be a negative or positive experience.

Administrative Styles

There are different styles of administration which operate differently to attain the same desired goals. There are four distinctly different administrative roles. They are as follows: (1) Autocratic (2) Democratic (3) Participatory (4) Bureaucratic.

1. **Autocratic**
    The autocratic leader takes authority and enjoys a challenge. He is usually a good manager. The autocratic leader has the ability to make hard decisions in a timely manner.

2. **Democratic**
    A democratic leader has the ability to motivate groups and individuals. His ability to articulate effectively is a positive asset. The democratic leader promotes team management but retains the authority to make the final decisions.

3. **Participatory**
    This type of leader is focused and has a corporate attitude. He is a good listener and is effective as the facilitator. He possesses the strong attribute of delegation.

4. **Bureaucratic**
    A person using this style in leading is usually analytical. This person is a crucial thinker and focuses on key details. This type of leader demands obedience and respect for authority.

All pastors have a particular style of management or leadership. It is not my intent to evaluate their effectiveness or rate one style over the other. Each of these styles of management has been used successfully by pastors. As we examine the different modes of management, it does seem that the preference of pastors is more often an autocratic or bureaucratic style. The personality of pastors often determines the style of leadership which is used.

It is interesting to note that some administrators are able to shift from one style to another depending upon the situation at hand. I was appointed to a church which had an average attendance of 175 and was somewhat self-sufficient.

During the previous 20 years, the church had had five different pastors. Because of the frequent changes, a void developed in pastoral leadership. Because of this lack of consistent leadership, the chairman of the board, who had a very strong personality, assumed the primary leadership position in the church. He made arbitrary decisions without approval of the boards or church conferences. Much was accomplished in church improvements and acquisition of properties, although the membership had limited knowledge of how these things were accomplished. But very little was accomplished in church growth during these 20 years. It appeared that the officers and members were reluctant or even fearful to hold the pastor accountable for the decisions that were made.

As I became more aware of this situation, it became obvious that this arrangement was not helpful in promoting church growth or making disciples. This was not a healthy situation.

We refer to the church as the body of Christ, and this implies that the church is a living organism. Recall that healthy churches grow, and unhealthy churches decline. Living organisms are susceptible to certain illnesses that impair their normal functions. To bring about change in this condition, it would require serious thought and planning because of the sensitive nature of the situation.

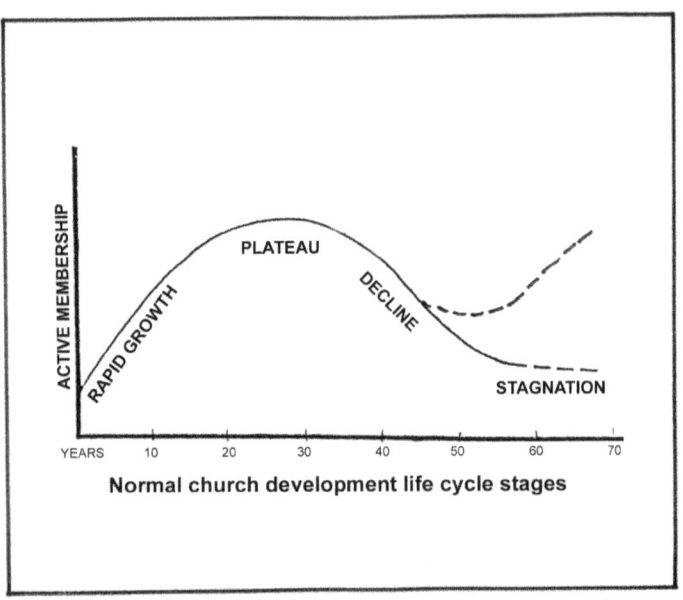

Normal church development life cycle stages

As churches age there is a tendency to enter a decline. In order to stop the decline there has to be an intervention of events to cause an incline in growth again. The broken line indicates that some type of event has occurred to stimulate growth again.

After giving serious thought to this situation, I decided not to approach it directly. Instead, my decision was to continue reinforcing my relationships with the other board members. During this process, I suggested the names of two individuals who I thought would make an excellent board chairperson. At the end of the conference year, one of these individuals was elected as chairman of the board. Even though the chairman was unexpectedly surprised at the results of the election, the problem was solved without any confrontation or hard feelings. The results of this process cleared the way for other changes that had to be made for this church to become a healthy body of Christ.

Let us not assume that all situations can be solved without anger or a great amount of resistance. Depending upon prevailing circumstances, sometimes the authoritative approach may be a more effective approach to management.

Principle #4: The leadership strength of the pastor and favorable transition of pastors is a prime factor in growing a church

Pastor-Lay Relationships

My approach in dealing with clergy-lay relationships is based on several years of service as a pastor and church consultant. I learned early as a pastor that I had to market my skills. When I became a consultant, I knew that I would have to market myself. I entered the consulting business where I would have to market my skills.

Pastors must be concerned with the needs of the members; they must pay attention and listen to them. The consultant has to learn to listen to clients in order to understand their real needs. Clients usually articulate certain needs, although the needs they have stated are not always the real needs. The consultant, through experience, is able to understand what the real needs are.

Consultants are perceived by their clients as being uniquely qualified as a professional. This idea was driven home as I was in a session with my editor. She questioned why I was exercising certain constraints in the way I worded a particular statement. My explanation was somewhat vague, and she was immediately able to perceive that I was being very careful of my choice of words in stating my position. She said, "Rev. Tollette, you are the professional, and you have the expertise to state in no uncertain terms whatever you believe as it relates to church consultation." I learned very early that the many challenges I would meet in my consultations would require that I present myself as an authority with the expertise to solve problems which pastors and congregations are confronted with.

Problem Solving Through Consultation

The ideal relationship between the laity and clergy should be congenial when working together toward the common goal of bringing the Good News to the unchurched and unsaved. Unfortunately, sometimes there is a certain amount of tension between the laity and clergy. Strong leadership by the pastor usually will reduce or eliminate the problem. There may be a question of what is meant by the phrase "strong leadership." It seems as if it means different things to different people. Simply stated, a strong leader is one who leads effectively. However, the process of leading may be complicated.

Successful managers always surround themselves with a small group of people who are frequently called the "inner circle." When consulting with churches, I usually suggest forming this small group and designate it as the "administrative council." The name implies that it is organized with the intent to empower the members to assume a more direct management role in decision making and planning.

Those chosen to be members of this group have demonstrated trust and loyalty over a period of time. Members chosen to serve on the administrative council must possess certain gifts and talents which would be helpful in making administrative decisions. Members of the council are highly respected by the congregation and wield a great amount of influence. Even though these persons possess these positive attributes of influence and respect, it may be necessary that they be empowered to function as managers.

We concluded that the best way to empower the members of the council is by developing their leadership potential. To this end, we considered setting up a leadership academy to train them in the art of leadership. It was at this time that John Maxwell, the foremost expert on leadership, extended an invitation to our church to bring our leadership team to his headquarters in Atlanta, Georgia, for an audience with him and his leadership team. We were completely overwhelmed when we received this offer from one of the most renowned individual teaching leadership and church finance. Needless to say, we were honored to accept this offer immediately and learned much from his experience.

What Is a Consultation?

Consultation is a process where a qualified person with the necessary expertise provides insights and recommendations that will help the church accomplish its mission. The consultant helps the church to function according to the biblical mandates as stated in the book of Acts 2:42–47. I can state with certainty that church development or church growth is related to numbers—

the number of new members, the number of baptisms, and the number of ministries. Church health is related to how well the church functions in fulfilling God's mission.

There are numerous instances in the Old and New Testament where effective advice and counsel were given. The last command Jesus gave to his disciples before his ascension was, "Go ye therefore and make disciples of all nations, baptizing them in the name of the Father, and of the Son, and of the Holy Ghost, teaching them to observe all things whatsoever I have commanded you: and lo, and I am with you always, even unto the end of the world" (Matthew 28:19–20).

Certain problems eventually come up in churches that the pastor is not equipped to handle. A person is needed who has undergone extensive training to help pastors and congregations solve these critical problems that they may be facing. Churches need help when there are specific issues within the congregation which are usually serious, such as:

1. Attendance has reached a plateau or is declining
2. A decline in tithes and offerings
3. Visitors do not return or join the church
4. Conflict within the church—between pastoral leadership and lay leadership or even between different groups within the congregation
5. Assistance needed in the process of merging congregations

Effective administrators are usually able to solve most of these problems although items two, four, and five will usually require the services of a consultant. Many churches do not have a plan ensuring growth, either short term or long term. Therefore, they need help in designing and implementing a plan for growth. A church may be functioning relatively well, but they may not have a reliable assessment of their strengths and weaknesses.

One of the most challenging and difficult situations a pastor has to deal with is the problem of merging two congregations into one. I will share an incident where I was called upon to intervene in a situation where the pastor was struggling to bring two congregations together.

In the summer of 2007, Bullock Temple CME Church, Little Rock, Arkansas, embarked on a journey to renew itself and reestablish its community as a unified community of believers. When Pastor Logan was assigned pastor of Bullock Temple, a congregation accompanied him to this new assignment. This immediately became a major problem of assimilation into the congregation. The previous pastor, Pastor Hampton, had instituted an 8 A.M. contemporary worship service to compliment the 10:45 A.M. traditional service. Although the 8 A.M. service attracted members and worshipers, the church did not experience significant numerical growth. In fact, there was concern that the church had become "two churches in one location."

To move the church beyond this impasse, the pastor invited me to come in and work with church leaders and members to chart a new course. My first consultation took place over the course of five days. The teaching sessions focused on vision, church pathology, church growth, and leadership. At the conclusion, the church developed a vision and mission statement which served to point the church in a strategic direction.

The vision statement reads as follows:
"We are a Christian family committed to
  Worship God
  Study the Word of God
  Work for God and
  Witness for God."

The new mission statement expanded the understanding of the vision statement:

1. To offer dynamic, exciting, Spirit-filled worship opportunities for the generations

2. To be a Word-centered body of believers committed to studying, learning, and living God's Word

3. To prepare and send forth Christian workers to transform the church and the community through their work

4. To witness for Christ in effective and creative ways

Further, the mission included the following:

1. To offer dynamic, exciting, Spirit-filled worship opportunities for the generations
   - Family life center
   - Youth minister dedicated to youth w/separate service
   - Make church property inviting
   - Greeters from parking lot to pew
   - More diverse worship
   - Enhanced music ministry

2. To be a Word-centered body of believers committed to studying, learning, and living God's Word
   - Biblical life application courses: money management, etc.
   - Leadership development training
   - Discipleship training

3. To prepare and send forth Christian workers to transform the church and the community through their work
   - Youth services and ministries: tutoring, mentoring, assist unwed mothers, dance classes, Bible Study
   - Children, young adult, singles, and elderly ministries
   - Purchase property across the street
   - Networking with church resources: directory of gifts
   - Food and clothing ministry
   - Monthly and annual activities: bowling, movie night, missions

4. To witness for Christ in effective and unique ways
   - Recording studio
   - Comprehensive program from cradle to grave
   - Work to eliminate racial problems
   - Meet needs of people in the community

To ensure that the vision and mission statements would be actualized, the pastor and leader developed an implementation timeline.
   - July
     o Recruit vision partners

- Build worship team
  - Hire worship minister/minister of music
  - Establish prayer ministry
- August
  - Mini-leadership retreat
  - Teach discipleship class
  - Establish a media ministry team
- September
  - Establish a web presence
  - Invite the community and send promotional materials
  - Worship rehearsal
- October
  - Launch New Bullock Temple
  - Commence planning for the children and youth worship services
  - Spiritual Gifts retreat/workshop

Following the workshops, it was suggested the church initiate a 9:30 A.M. unity service which eliminated the 8 A.M. and 10:45 A.M. worship services. The new service was well received, and it solved the usual problems associated with the merger of two congregations. The music was blended, and the worship experience was intergenerational. Hiring a new music director made it possible to develop worship that met diverse needs.

In addition, new members brought the necessary leadership and understanding of the vision to fully implement aspects of the mission statement. The children's ministry now hosts a worship service for children 3–5 years old and 6–11 years old. The children's ministry conducts five Day Clubs in the summer and Good News Clubs during the school year.

The youth ministry has continued to grow. We have developed a youth and young adult choir, YAYA, which is full of the Spirit, has wonderful energy, and has increased youth and young adult participation in worship. The youth department caught fire. Youth participate in the Wednesday night Bible Study, Sunday School, YAYA choir, usher board, and the praise dance team. The youth's Wednesday night Bible Study is well attended. The youth set goals to become more knowledgeable in the Word of God and to give back to the church and community. Further, the church has partnered with Young Life, which brings unchurched students to the church each week to hear about the grace and goodness of our Lord and Savior, Jesus Christ.

The past three years have been most exciting and very busy. All the "newness" was generally well received, but we did lose some members. However, on any given Sunday, a visitor is likely to see others in their generation among the 100 or so folks that worship with us. We have much work to do to continue to discern and do God's will in this part of God's vineyard.

EXERCISE

Pastors must understand the threefold responsibility of pastoring. It is:

1. _____
2. _____
3. _____

When a proposal is rejected by the board or the congregation, there are three options available. They are:

1. _____
2. _____
3. _____

Chapter 11

PRAYER

Today, we are living in a busy world. We go shopping, drive on the freeways, we hurry to work and hurry back home. As a result of all of our rushing, we end up as prisoners of our ambitions. I was employed by the Los Angeles Unified School District, attending seminary two evenings a week and pastoring a church. One Sunday morning as I approached the summit of the Cajon Pass, I noticed a large sign on a restaurant with a statement that read, "Open 25 hours a day." I said to myself that this is just what I need, one more hour in the day and I would be able to do all of the things on my agenda. Then I began to think of how much time I had spent in prayer. Then, through a brief introspection of my busy activities, I immediately realized I was negligent in taking enough time out to pray.

The numerical and spiritual increase in the local body of believers is the result of calling upon the Holy Spirit. The church is God's creation; Jesus Christ is its head. The church is a living organism which grows through prayer and involvement. James states, "… The factual fervent prayer of a righteous man availeth much in its working" (James 5:16). Paul wrote, "I planted the seed, Apollo watered, but God made it grow" (I Corinthians 3:6). A seed can be planted in the ground, watered, pruned, cared for; but the growth is a result of something supernatural and mysterious. This is a wonderful process that takes place underground independent of human will or hands. So it is with the church.

The Psalmist stated, "Unless the Lord builds the church, its builders labor in vain" (Psalms 127:1). Nothing of lasting value can be accomplished in programming, in finance, or in organization, unless all things are done in prayer. If we are convinced growth comes from God and is therefore supernatural, and if we are equally convinced that we are dependent on him for lasting results, then prayer will be at the top of the priority list. If God causes growth, then we must be in touch with him.

The power behind the church is the power of the Holy Spirit. It is the Holy Spirit who calls us to faith. The power of God's spirit is what helps people to grow in discipleship. This is what took place at Pentecost (Acts 2:1). Often, we stand in the way of God in his effort to carry out his plan to save those who have not accepted him as Savior. It is through prayer that man is able to clear the channel so that the Holy Spirit may be able to minister. This is what took place at Pentecost (Acts 2:1) when the apostles and the followers of Jesus Christ displayed a new commitment, a new understanding, and a new vision for God's purposes.

God loves his church, and he is always ready to make his resources available to us, but he sometime waits for us to ask. We talk about prayer, but we do not make it our number-one priority.

We busy ourselves doing creative programming, structuring, and organizing, building expensive and beautiful facilities, and we often do these things without the deep sense of need of the Lord. Such an attitude toward prayer may be the result of a tendency to measure results in a different way than God does. We measure the number of people, the amount of dollars, size of our facilities, who belongs to our church, etc. God is concerned about these things, but he measures results in a different way. He looks at the condition of our hearts. He is concerned about unconfessed sin, and whether we love God and each other, whether we care about those who are lost. These are situations which he alone can deal with in answering our prayers.

God is at work in the inner part of man's heart and in his life. The apostle Paul gave us models for our prayers. He prayed that God's people would develop those spiritual qualities that are of great importance. Paul prayed for a deepening love between believers, for a clearer understanding of who Jesus is, and for increased patience as God answers in tribulation and persecution. We began to see things of significance happening as God answers our prayers. Praying will then become more than an optional program for the faithful few, and instead, will become a driving force in all of our lives.

In order that prayer may be elevated to the position of prominence in our churches, various opportunities for prayer involvement on an individual and corporate level must be initiated. There are three primary tasks: (1) teaching the rules of prayer, (2) modeling a lifestyle of prayer, and (3) organizing and programming for prayer.

Praying with Faith

The first rule of prayer is one must pray with faith. The Christian must believe that God will answer prayer. The more we are convinced that what we are praying for is God's will, the stronger our faith grows. The Bible is replete with scriptures that serve to increase our faith. This is attested to by the scriptures, "Faith is the substance of things hoped for, the evidence of things not seen" (Hebrews 11:1). And also, "This is the confidence that we have in him, that if we ask anything according to his will, he hears us" (I John 5:14). As we become more knowledgeable of the scriptures, our faith grows stronger.

Another rule to remember is to pray with a clean heart. We should examine our hearts constantly to make sure that we are making every effort to live a life of holiness as we ask God to answer our prayers. The scripture teaches "… Ye shall be holy: for I the Lord your God am holy" (Leviticus 19:2). "Sanctify yourselves therefore, and be ye holy …" (Leviticus 20:7). Yes, every Christian should be sanctified.

Whenever we pray, we should pray with power. Jesus said to his disciples, "But ye shall receive power, after that the Holy Ghost comes upon you …" (Acts 1:7). We receive that power as we are filled with the Holy Spirit. The question is, "How do we know when we are filled with the Holy Spirit?" Many Christians have offered elaborate explanations detailing how we receive the Holy Spirit. This results in a very complicated understanding of the Holy Spirit and how we receive him. Some people feel that all they have to do is go through the four spiritual laws and accept

Jesus as their Savior. Others feel that there has to be some kind of visible display or sign indicating that a person is filled with the Holy Spirit. I believe that a person has to simply ask God to fill him with the Holy Spirit. When one is filled with the Holy Spirit, his life should reflect a strong prayer life. Some people have the spiritual gift of intercessory prayer, and this gift is evidenced by praying for other people.

God's desire is to carry out his plan of salvation and growth of his church. It is through prayer that man is able to clear the channel so that the Holy Spirit may be able to minister. This is what took place at Pentecost (Acts 2:1) when the apostles and the followers received a new understanding and a new vision for God's purposes. God loves his church and stands ready to make his resources available to us, but he sometime waits for us to ask.

PRAYER: An Essential for Church Growth

"The effective, fervent prayer of a righteous man availeth much" (James 5:16).

Many authors have written books on principles of church growth, and it is surprising that prayer isn't given enough consideration. Prayer must be the foundation of any endeavor or undertaking by the cooperate body of the church, and most certainly by individuals. Much is said about prayer, but it seems that the talk does not always translate into active prayer ministries.

I have attended many events under the guise of prayer breakfasts, but prayer wasn't always the primary focus at these events. It is not my intent to demean in any way this event because much is accomplished which has a positive impact on the lives of persons through prayer breakfasts.

Materials which explain in detail how to organize prayer ministries apparently are scarce or difficult to find. As a result, we are not aware of how this affects church growth.

There is one thing consistent with growing churches, and that is the prayer life of the pastor. Church growth pastors devote a great amount of time in private prayer. Not only do they have an effective personal prayer life, but they usually have an organized prayer ministry that involves the whole congregation.

One of the best ways of learning how to develop a stronger personal prayer life is by talking to pastors who have strong prayer lives. One can learn more about establishing an effective prayer ministry by talking to pastors who have developed an effective prayer ministry in their congregation. Remember, it doesn't belittle or demean one to seek help from those who may have more expertise in areas where you may be somewhat lacking. I'll share an example of a young pastor who has made a tremendous impact on my prayer life.

Pastor James Markham arrived at this small desert town of Victorville, California, some 28 years ago to pastor Emmanuel Temple Church. Emmanuel Temple was a congregation of approximately 250 members when he was assigned as pastor. Today, this congregation has a true membership of over 2,000.

The unique aspect of his ministry is a strong personal prayer life. He spends at least two hours each day in prayer, seeking God's guidance and blessings for his church and members. This pastor has an unusual commitment to prayer. It is difficult to categorize or adequately describe this pastor's leadership style. One thing is apparent, however. His style of leadership has been unusually successful. This is borne out by the many accomplishments that have taken place during his tenure of 28 years.

His demeanor is rather easygoing and evidences a deep love for his members. He has a certain command of his congregation which is easily recognized. His accomplishments include building a new sanctuary and liquidating the mortgage within five years and the purchase of ten more acres of land. An outstanding feature about him is that Pastor Markham was a visionary and was able to instill this vision in the hearts of the members.

It isn't unusual that pastors have a vision from God, but are unable to instill it in their congregation. Why is it that many pastors are unsuccessful in implementing their vision? I do believe that the missing factor is *prayer*. Pastor Markham understands that all ministries must be fortified by prayer. We sometimes neglect to consider prayer as the prime factor of efficient leadership.

There are many opportunities available for learning more about developing personal prayer ministries. It may be expedient for pastors to take advantage by attending seminars and conferences sponsored by mega-churches or para-church organizations. Conferences and seminars of this type are more effective simply because more time is available to teach one discipline. Many seminars of this type are available in all areas of the country.

An excellent seminar on prayer, which I highly recommend, is sponsored by the World Prayer Center in Colorado Springs. Dr.

Peter Wagner, a professor of church growth at Fuller Seminary, is one of the founders of this center.

Serving as a consultant for Phillips Temple Church in Dayton, Ohio, I arranged to send several members of our prayer ministry to attend a prayer seminar in Colorado Springs. The information and training they received was extremely helpful in developing an effective prayer ministry at Phillips Temple. Today, our church offers many opportunities for its members to be engaged in prayer events. To this end, Phillips Temple has added a staff position of director of Prayer Ministry, whose responsibility is to coordinate prayer events in the church and selected areas of the community wherever the need exists. A men's prayer group meets each Saturday morning from eight until nine. After the prayer session, the men do visitation to the homes of individuals who are sick or incapacitated. A women's prayer group also meets at the same hour.

Each fifth Sunday, an intercessory prayer group retreats to a special room to pray for the pastor during the eight and eleven A.M. worship services. Special prayer times are scheduled for couples, parents, children, and youth. Once a month, there is a regular prayer vigil scheduled in the sanctuary on Fridays between the hours of nine P.M. and one A.M. All of these prayer events are well attended.

Why Should We Pray?

The scriptures teach us that *everything* we undertake, individually or corporately, must be fortified by prayer. Jesus stated this idea in a parable. "... Men ought to always pray, and not faint" (Luke 18:1). Pastors and members should devote an adequate amount of time in prayer. When I speak of time in prayer it must be understood that it isn't only the *amount* of the time spent in prayer; it also should be *quality* time.

We should pray because we have an invitation from Jesus when he said, "Ask and it shall be given, seek and ye shall find, knock and the door shall be opened unto you" Matthew 7.

We should pray because prayer glorifies God! "I will do whatever you ask in my name, so that the father may be glorified" (Jn. 14:13).

We should pray in order to experience the closeness of God. "The Lord is near to all who call on him in truth" (Psalm 145:18).

We should pray in order to experience the forgiveness of God. "If my people pray, seek my face, and turn from their wicked ways, then I will hear from heaven, and will forgive their sin and heal their land" (2 Chronicles 7:14).

EXERCISE

1. What are three primary tasks to make prayer a high priority?

    a. _____

    b. _____

    c. _____

2. Complete the following sentence.

    When one is filled with the _____
    his life should reflect a strong _____
    _____.

Chapter 12

ASSIMILATING NEW MEMBERS

One of the most difficult and challenging problems for churches is developing an effective assimilation ministry for new members. The objective of the assimilation ministry should be that those who have joined recently will become active and responsible members of the church, disciples of Christ.

Sometimes individuals who attend regularly show all the qualities of a member before they actually join. In other words, these persons are functioning as members before they officially unite with the church.

The most important contact when people visit or unite with the church is the Assimilation Ministry. The purpose of this ministry is to help others understand the dynamics of membership. The assimilation process begins when visitors arrive on the church parking lot. Jesus makes this very plain to his disciples when he met on a mountain in Galilee after his resurrection. He spoke these words: "Go ye therefore, and teach all nations, baptizing them in the name of the Father, and of the Son, and of the Holy

Ghost, teaching them to observe all things whatsoever I have commanded you: and lo, I am with you always, even unto the end of the world."

The purpose of assimilation is to help people understand the responsibilities of membership. Assimilation is a process which helps the new member become an active member of the church. Some people attend the church on a regular basis but have not officially joined. Many of these individuals may be involved in small groups such as the choir or usher board in the church. They may be considered prospective members. Experience has shown that many of these persons drop out after a period of time, perhaps because they have not made a full commitment to the church. New people don't just become members by walking down the aisle and joining the church. They must go through the process of assimilation which will take a considerable amount of time. Even after they unite with the church, many of them will become inactive soon after they have joined. This is why it is important that the church have an assimilation ministry.

The first level of inactivity is the "inactive member." These people might be in worship once a month or on special days such as Christmas, Mother's Day, and Easter. These members still consider the minister for weddings, funerals, and special needs. They may give financially, but they have no real commitment of time or involvement in the church. If there's no strategy in place to involve these inactive members in the ministries of the church they will eventually drop out permanently. At this stage, they are on their way to the "back door." If this limited participation continues, they will eventually drop out completely. The longer a member has dropped out, the more difficult it is to reactivate him/her. Every church should have within their Evangelism Department an Attendance Committee. It is the duty of this committee to monitor the involvement of members for signs of inactivity and attendance.

Conclusions Concerning Assimilation

Assimilation just doesn't happen on its own. Many things make it difficult to assimilate new members. A well planned assimilation ministry is necessary to overcome these difficulties. Older members (those who have been members of the church for a longer period of time) believe that they are friendly toward new members, but their actions may say otherwise. Older members must see the church through the eyes of a new member. Oftentimes it is difficult for newer members to feel comfortable in the existing small groups in the church. Older members seem to wait for the new member to use their initiative to join a small group. The new member expects the old members to take the initiative to encourage them to join a particular ministry. One church solved this problem by having chairpersons of the various groups come to the new member orientation class to explain their ministries and extend an invitation for them to join their group.

Even though the Attendance Committee has the primary responsibility of assimilating new members, it is also the task for every member of the church. When new members join the church, they do not expect to become inactive or drop out. The cause of dropping out or inactivity is apparently related to the effectiveness of the assimilation process. Assimilation should begin before they join the church and continue on afterward. When people join the church, it is usually because of the friendships which existed prior to joining that church. Everyone has a circle of friends, of which some may be saved or unsaved. These prior friendships sometimes determine whether a person stays and becomes involved after becoming a member.

Research points out that 75–80 percent of all members who become inactive do so within six months or a year after joining. It is not always newer members who drop out. Sometimes longtime members may drop out simply because they experience burnout; in other words, they just get tired. The chairperson of the Assimilation Committee must be able to determine whether there should be a change in the committee positions.

There are differences between older members and newer members. New members usually join the church because of a personal need being met or because needs are met through the worship service and/or the different ministries that are offered. Older members have established meaningful relationships over a period of time in the church which meets their needs. Newer members tend to be more optimistic and enthusiastic about the church compared to the older members. Most new members feel like outsiders and find it difficult to acquire a sense of belonging, whereas the older members are long-established in the church. There are many other differences in the older and newer members, but these differences are touched upon throughout other sections of the book.

The goal of the assimilation ministry is to provide an opportunity for new members to become actively involved in the activities of the church. You might say this ministry serves the purpose of "opening the front door, and closing the back door." Therefore, all churches should have an active assimilation ministry, not just in name only. As previously mentioned, many persons become active in the church even before they join. Others become active after they have joined. Unfortunately, many who have joined the church become inactive or drop out very soon after joining. One of the factors which determines the health of the church is the percentage of active members. The primary responsibility of assimilating new members into the church remains with the assimilation ministry. However, it's worth reiterating that even though the primary responsibility remains with this ministry, *every member* must play a part in assimilating members.

The Assimilation Ministry

The effectiveness of the committee depends on how it is structured. It should be structured in such a way that it covers several areas which are necessary for an effective assimilation ministry. There are five areas that must be considered in structuring the committee. These areas are (1) Prayer, (2) Prospect, (3) Visitation, (4) Preparatory, and (5) Attendance. It is not unusual that churches may organize this committee differently. Many churches have added to the above five committees. No matter what configuration is used, the committee must be structured to accomplish the objective of assimilating new members into the church.

Every endeavor that the church is involved in must be undergirded with prayer. The prayer committee organizes prayer events both inside and outside the church. The prayer committee will pray for the success of every activity the church is involved in.

Everyone on the assimilation ministry must remember that a visitor must be welcomed into the church in a friendly and helpful way. If the first impression of the church is a negative one, it is unlikely that the visitor will return for a second time. When people drive onto the church parking they should be met by attendants or greeters. Greeters will direct the visitors and members to convenient parking places. These men are easily recognized as they wear bright colored vests. Members of this committee are also equipped with umbrellas when there is inclement weather. Visitors are then escorted to the entrance of the church where they are met by another group of greeters stationed at all entrances of the church. These greeters will inform the visitors of the floor plan of the church, such as restrooms, nursery, nurse's station, etc. The visitors are then directed to the Information Center where they will receive a brochure containing information about ministries of the church and its core values.

From this point they are escorted into the sanctuary by the ushers and seated next to a member of the church who will explain what is taking place in the worship. It should not be taken for granted that visitors understand what is happening in the worship service. This process assures that the visitor is not left alone from the time he/she arrives on the campus until after the benediction has been pronounced. Churches which have a number of visitors each Sunday will usually offer a treat after service. This makes a positive impression on the visitor, and they will not forget the hospitality which was shown.

Principle #9: Friendliness of a congregation assures growth

Most churches will place an information card in the bulletin. Generally the pastor will ask the guests to fill it out and place it in the offering tray. If the church doesn't use this method it is important that they find another nonthreatening way to gather this information from the first-time guests. This is the best way to receive information from the visitor so that follow-up can be made. The prospect committee should meet on the Monday following Sunday worship service and contact the first-time visitors with a phone call. If the first-time visitors indicated that they have e-mail, the first contact could be made by e-mail. The first-time visitors should be contacted as soon as possible after the Sunday service as this encourages them to visit the church for a second time.

The second contact should be made 36 hours after visiting the church. The second contact is a card expressing our appreciation that they chose our church to worship at. These contacts serve to convince the visitor that the members of this church are friendly and open to visitors. When visitors return to the church a second time, the focus should be to encourage that person to become a regular attendee. The second-time guest will be asked to fill out an information card which will provide information on how they may participate in ministries. This is an effective way for visitors to get involved in ministries such as small groups, walking, aerobics, and bowling. This approach creates a sense of personal ownership in the church.

When a visitor begins to attend on a regular basis, he/she will usually develop a sense of ownership, pride, and identification with the church. At this stage, members should cease insisting that the attendee become a member of the church because it is obvious that he has an interest in the church. During this period, the attendee is establishing significant relationships with members and assuming some responsibilities within the church. The attendee must develop a friendship with at least seven persons. The attendee will cease to say, "This is the church I attend" and will begin to say, "This is my church." The visitor is no longer just a "consumer"; he/she has now become a "participant."

New members and attendees will be informed about different opportunities for service in the church. They are informed by letter or e-mail that attendees may attend the new member classes and participate in other small group ministries. They will be taught about the requirements of membership and baptism, the history of the church, its beliefs, core values, and a brief survey of the Bible. After a person has completed the membership class, he/she is required to sign the Membership Covenant to become a member.

INFORMATION CARD

Mr./ Mrs./ Ms./ Miss
Name: _____
Address: _____
City: _____ State: _____ Zip:_____
Phone ( )_____ Email: _____
Iama: [ ] 1st time guest [ ] 2nd time guest [ ] Regular: Attendee [ ] Member
___ How to form a relationship with Jesus Christ
___ Information on Small Groups
___ Information on Baptism
___ Information on Church Membership
___ Participating any way I can in the Church
___ I would like information about New Member Classes
Comments or Prayer Requests: _____
_____
_____
_____

If 1st or 2nd time guest: How did you hear about our Church?
(Circle One)
Flyer - Newspaper - Postcard -
Name of person who invited you: _____

Please place this card in the offering Tray or hand it to an Usher

EXERCISE

1. The objective of the assimilation committee is to see that those who have joined the church will become _____ and _____ members of the church.

2. Older members think that they are friendly, but their actions may show that they are not _____.

3. Research points out that 75 percent to 85 percent of all members who become inactive do so within six to twelve _____ after joining.

Conclusion

Throughout this book I have approached the subject of church growth from the perspective of 10 church growth principles. The objective or goals of the church is to make disciples. This is the mandate which Jesus stated in Matthew 28:19–20. Therefore, this must be the objective of every activity that the church is engaged in. There are many principles of church growth which could be used, but I have chosen 10 of these principles which I have applied successfully in growing churches as a pastor. These principles have also been used in consulting with various churches. By applying these 10 principles, churches will grow. You will find that as your church grows it will become an exciting venture when you see your pews being filled to the maximum.

I have sought to spell out the meaning of church growth principles and how they are used to grow your church. Churches will benefit greatly by using these principles. As was stated earlier, this was not intended to be an academic endeavor. Instead, it was designed as a "How To ..." approach to accomplish the mandate of making disciples. It is my hope that these principles will become operative in the life of any congregation that desires to reach the unsaved. Church growth principles, when executed, cause the church to move from where it is to where God desires it to be.

Bibliography

1. Benjamin, Paul. *The Growing Congregation*. Standard Publishing, 1972.
   This book explores the basic principles of church growth as related to the activities in other American churches.
2. Buttry, Daniel. *Bringing Your Church Back To Life*. Judson Press, Valley Forge, PA, 1988.
3. Cho, Paul (with R. Whitney Manzano). *More Than Numbers*. World Books Publisher, Waco, Texas, 1984.
4. Downey, Marray W. *The Art of Soul-Winning*. Baker Book House, Grand Rapids, 1957; Seventh printing, May 1983.
5. Elliott, Ralph H. *Church Growth That Counts*. Judson Press, Valley Forge, PA 19481, 1982.
   This book takes an honest look at the church growth movement and principles and re-evaluates them in the light of biblical principles.
6. Hanks, Billy Jr. *Everyday Evangelism*. The Zondervan Corporation, Grand Rapids, Michigan, 1983.
7. Hinkle, Herbert J. *How To Reach Multitudes For Christ*. New Hope Press, 1979, Grand Rapids, Michigan.
   A successful black pastor in Inkster, Michigan, who has experienced phenomenal growth in his church.
8. Hinkle, Herbert J. *Soul Winning In Black Churches*. Baker Book House, Grand Rapids, Michigan; Fifth printing, 1982.

9. Hunter, George C. *The Contagious Congregation—Frontiers in Evangelism and Church Growth.* The Parthenon Press, 1979.
   This book addresses the number-one problem in mainline and traditional denominations and congregations.

10. Hunter, Kent R. *Foundations of Church Growth.* Leader Publishing Co., 1983, New Haven.
    An excellent introduction to church growth; it is both comprehensive and extensive.

11. Jenson, Ron, and Jim Stevens. *Dynamics of Church Growth.* Baker Book House, Grand Rapids, Michigan, 1981.

12. Kelluy, Dean M. *Why Conservative Churches Are Growing.* Harper & Row Publishers, New York, 1977.
    This book clears up some of the existing confusion about what can be expected of religion and under what conditions. It is highly recommended.

13. McGarvran, Donald A. & Winfield C. Arn. *Ten Steps To Church Growth.* Harper & Row, 1977.

14. McGarvran, Donald A. & Winfield C. Arn. *How To Grow A Church.* G/L Publishers, Glendale, CA 91209, 1975.

15. Miles, Delos. *Church Growth: A Mighty River.* Broadman Press, Nashville, Tenn., 1981.
    An overview of the movement from its beginnings to the present. The church growth movement is likened to a river that has widened its area of influence. This book will help put the movement in proper perspective.

16. Moore, Waylon B. *Multiplying Disciples—The New Testament Method For Church Growth.* NavPress, Colorado Springs, 1981.
    This book offers practical guidelines for pastors and laymen on starting disciple-making ministries in their local church.

17. Schaller, Lyie E. *Activating The Passive Church: Diagnosis & Treatment*. Abingdon Press, Nashville, TN, 1981.

18. Schaller, Lyie E. *Growing Plans: Strategies To Increase Your Church's Membership*. Abingdon Press, 1983.
Five different strategies are developed for increasing the size of the congregation. These strategies are adaptable to small, middle-sized, and larger congregations. The author also discusses denominational strategies.

19. Schaller, Lyie E. Creative Leadership Series, *Assimilating New Members*. Abingdon Press, Nashville, TN 1978; Eleventh printing, 1984.

20. Schuller, Robert. *Move Ahead With Possibility Thinking*. Spire Books, Fleming H. Revell Company, Old Tappan, N.J. 1967.

21. Schuller, Robert. *The Greatest Possibility Thinker That Ever Lived*. Fleming H. Revell Company, 1973.

22. Schuller, Robert. *Your Church Has Real Possibilities*. Regal Books, 1974, Ventura, CA.

23. Schuller, Robert. *Discover Your Possibilities*. Harvest House Publishers, Eugene, Oregon 97402.
Smith, Donald P. *Congregations Alive*. Westminster Press, Philadelphia, 1981.
A probing examination of what active congregations are like, how they got that way, and what style of pastoral and lay leadership stimulated and nurtured them.

24. Snyder, Howard A. *The Radical Wesley & Patterns for Church Renewal*. InterVarsity Press, Downers Grove, 1L. 60515, 1980.

25. Wagner, C. Peter. *Church Growth and the Whole Gospel: A Biblical Mandate*. Harper & Row Publishers, San Francisco, CA 1981.
This book attempts to answer criticism and to show

more clearly how the church growth movement does support the whole gospel.

26. Southerland, Dan. *Transitioning*. Zondervan Publishing House, Grand Rapids, MI 1999.

27. Wagner, C. Peter. *Leading Your Church To Growth*. G/L Publishers, Ventura, CA.
This book is narrowly focused on church membership growth for both clergy and laity.

28. Wagner. C. Peter. *Your Church Can Be Healthy*. Creative Leadership Series, Abingdon Press, Nashville. Lyle E. Schaller, Editor, 1979.

29. Wagner, C. Peter. *Your Church Can Grow: Seven Vital Signs Of A Healthy Church*. G/L Publications, Ventura, GA.
The author examines scientific measures of a church and what makes it grow or not grow.

30. Zunkel, C. Wayne. *Growing The Small Church: A Guide For Church Members*. David C. Cook Publishing Co., Elgin, IL 60120, 1983.
One of the most helpful sources for pastors and leaders of small churches. It focuses on churches with less than 200 members. Highly recommended!

31. Callahan, Kennon L. *Twelve Keys To An Effective Church— Strategic Planning For Mission*. Harper & Row Publishers, San Francisco, 1983.
This book is designed to assist local churches in their strategic long-range planning to be effective churches in mission. The author emphasizes the congregation's base as a starting point of planning.

32. Carroll, Jackson W. *Small Churches Are Beautiful*. Harper & Row Publishers, San Francisco, CA. 1977.
The author points out that over 50 percent of the major Protestant denominations have 200 members or less,

and the small church must be viewed as an entity in itself instead of a prototype of a larger church.

33. Rickard, Marvin G. *Let It Grow—Your Church Can Chart a New Course.* Multnomah Press, Portland, OR 97266, 1984.
Marvin Rickard came to pastor the 83-member Los Gatos, CA. church and some 25 years later, the membership has swelled to 6,500—one of the most dynamic and largest congregations in America.

34. Southard, Samuel. *Pastoral Evangelism.* John Knox Press, 1981, Atlanta, GA 30365.

PROGRAMS

1. Kennedy, D. James. *Evangelism Explosion.* The Coral Ridge Program For Lay Witness. Tyndale House Publishers, Wheaton, IL
This program has been in continuous operation in the Coral Ridge Presbyterian Church of Fort Lauderdale, Florida, for 15 years. Up to 500 lay witnesses have gone out weekly. It has grown to 4,500 members, with 11 full-time ministers on staff. A proven program.

2. Stephens, Kenneth. *Discipleship Evangelism.* Harvest House Publishers, Eugene, OR 97402, 1978.
This is a manual for evangelism through home Bible Studies, an approach which has proved itself in practice. Emphases are placed on making disciples.

3. Toilette, C.B. *Evangelism Workshop.* Ninth Episcopal District Dept. of Evangelism Christian Methodist Episcopal Church, Altadena CA.
An up-to-date practical and workable program for discipling members from the point of decision through the total process of becoming a disciple.

www.ingramcontent.com/pod-product-compliance
Lightning Source LLC
Chambersburg PA
CBHW020850090426
42736CB00008B/322